# EASY VEGETARIAN COOKING

## Sharon Cadwallader

BRISTOL PUBLISHING ENTERPRISES, INC.
San Leandro, California

# a nitty gritty® cookbook

Printed in the United States of America.

ISBN 1-55867-210-9

Cover design: Frank J. Paredes
Cover photography: John A. Benson
Food styling: Susan Massey
Illustrations: Shanti Nelson

# CONTENTS

For Pat and Terry

# EATING, VEGETARIAN-STYLE

As we approach the turn of the century, and in the wake of the healthy food revolution, many of us are adding more vegetarian dishes to our daily menus. Once upon a time, a vegetarian diet was considered odd and unhealthy, but cultural influences and medical insights have dispelled those notions. Now, health practitioners are recommending that we increase the number of vegetarian dishes in our diets. Of course, there are those who have come to feel philosophically and spiritually that they cannot eat animals in good conscience; others believe that the rapidly increasing population on this planet will simply not support the grazing land needed for feeding food animals. Whatever our personal beliefs or commitments, there is no question that at least a partial vegetarian diet is beneficial to our health and well-being.

Since plant sources, unlike animal sources, do not provide complete proteins, nutritionists have been concerned about getting enough protein in a vegetarian diet. However, recent studies show that the people in the United States generally take in far more protein than we need. Once we understand how to obtain complete proteins from a vegetarian diet, we can easily balance our own daily menus.

Proteins are made up of chains of *amino acids*, most of them created by our own bodies. However, some amino acids, called *essential amino acids*, must be obtained from the foods we eat. Animal protein sources contain all the essential amino acids, and are therefore considered *complete protein sources*. Most plant foods, however, are low in one or more of the essential amino acids, and are considered *incomplete protein sources*. To obtain complete protein from plant sources, one must combine different plant foods that have *complementary proteins* to create the proper amino acid balance. (One exception is soybeans, which contain all of the essential amino acids.) In other words, by combining one plant food, which is low in a certain essential amino acid, with another plant food, which is high in that particular amino acid, we can create a complete protein similar to that of an animal source.

This book is not *vegan*, which refers to a form of vegetarianism that does not include dairy products or eggs. As such, a good rule is to include daily helpings of milk products or eggs in the diet, which will make up for the limitations in vegetable protein.

We do not have to be scientists to eat well on a vegetarian diet, nor do we have to measure every gram of protein. Just keep in mind which plant sources complement each other and you will be eating well.

# TEIN CHART

*n creating your own vegetarian meals, this chart is helpful. Combine foods
fferent categories from columns 1, 2 and 3 to achieve balanced protein. Or,
y of the items from column 4 to guarantee a complete-protein meal.*

| COLUMN 1 | COLUMN 2 | COLUMN 3 | COLUMN 4 |
|---|---|---|---|
| **s:** | **Legumes:**<br>Dried beans, green peas, mung beans, peanuts | **Legumes:**<br>Dried beans, mung beans, peas, peanuts | **Dairy products:**<br>Cheese (except cream cheese, cottage cheese) Milk (including dry and canned), yogurt |
| **Grains:**<br>Barley, buckwheat, bulgur, cornmeal, millet, oats, rice, rye, wheat | **Nuts:**<br>Hazelnuts (filberts) | **Grains:**<br>Cornmeal | **Eggs:**<br>Whole and egg whites |
| **Nuts and seeds:**<br>Almonds, cashews, coconut, hazelnuts (filberts), pumpkin seeds, sunflower seeds, walnuts | **Vegetables:**<br>Asparagus, green beans, beet greens, broccoli, Brussels sprouts, mushrooms, parsley, green peas, potatoes, Swiss chard | **Nuts:**<br>English walnuts | **Legumes:**<br>Soybeans, soybean curd (tofu), soy flour, soy milk, tempeh |
| **Vegetables:**<br>Asparagus, beet greens, corn, kale, mushrooms, sweet potaotes, yams | | **Vegetables:**<br>Corn, beet greens mushrooms, green peas, Swiss chard | |

# SOUPS

# SOUPS IN A VEGETARIAN DIET

No vegetarian cookbook is quite complete without a soup section, especially since soups have grown in popularity over the past twenty years, not only as meal starters, but also as entrées. The soups in this section are varied: some are light and perfect for lunch or a first course; others are hearty and serve nicely as a main dish. Lentil soups, for example, make wonderful entrée soups. This chapter offers several for you to try. Potato soups are staples all around the world. Following are a few choices.

Because many vegetarian recipes call for a good vegetable stock, a standard recipe is offered. Make it once a week with the parings of your organically grown vegetables. Or, purchase a good-quality commercial brand of vegetable stock.

The amounts of salt called for in these recipes are mostly "to taste," as the saltiness of commercial stocks can vary widely. Season carefully: a savory stock makes a successful soup; a soup that's too salty is a disaster.

# VEGETABLE STOCK

*While there are many excellent commercial varieties of vegetable stock, you may wish to make your own. This basic recipe can be refrigerated for up to 4 days, or frozen for up to 1 month. If you normally use organically grown vegetables when preparing meals, it's nice to save their parings and add them to this stock with the vegetables. Parings can be kept in a plastic container or bag in the refrigerator for up to 4 days before using them.*

4 qt. water
4 large carrots, coarsely chopped
4 stalks celery, coarsely chopped
2 large onions, coarsely chopped
2 large potatoes, peeled and coarsely
   chopped

1 bunch fresh flat-leaf parsley, well
   washed
8 large cloves garlic, halved
15 peppercorns
vegetable parings, optional
2 bay leaves

In a large pot, combine water, carrots, celery, onions, potatoes, parsley, garlic, peppercorns, vegetable parings, if using, and bay leaves and bring to a boil. Reduce heat to low and simmer for 1½ hours. Cool stock slightly and strain through a fine sieve; discard vegetables.

# CARROT AND RICE SOUP WITH CUMIN

*This is a nice year-round soup that goes well with melted cheese sandwiches and a green salad. When choosing onions, look for flat ones, which tend to be sweeter than round ones.*

2 tbs. butter
1 large onion, preferably sweet, chopped
2 tsp. ground cumin
1 lb. carrots, peeled and sliced
1 cup sliced celery
2 cups water

3 cups *Vegetable Stock*, page 6 or
　　purchased, plus more if desired
⅓ cup uncooked white rice
salt and freshly ground pepper to taste
fresh flat-leaf parsley leaves for garnish

In a large pot, heat butter over medium heat and sauté onion for 4 minutes. Add cumin and sauté for 1 to 2 minutes. Add carrots, celery, water, stock and rice and bring to a boil. Reduce heat to low and simmer, covered, for about 10 minutes, until vegetables and rice are tender. Transfer mixture to a food processor workbowl or blender container and process until blended, but coarse in texture. Return mixture to pot, adding a little more stock if you desire a thinner soup. Season with salt and pepper and serve garnished with parsley leaves.

# BEET SOUP (BORSCHT)

*This easy soup can be made the day before you plan to serve it. In the summer, balance the protein by serving this soup chilled accompanied by melted cheese and tomato sandwiches on whole grain bread. In the winter, when you prefer a hot soup, complete the protein with egg salad or fried egg sandwiches, or **Tofu Burgers**, page 128. It's best not to strain this soup; a little thickness or fiber adds just the right satisfying texture to each spoonful.*

6 medium beets
2 tsp. olive oil
1 cup chopped onion
1¼ tsp. caraway seeds
3 cups water, plus more if desired
juice of 2 lemons, or more to taste
salt to taste
sour cream for garnish

Wash beets well. Trim green ends to 2 inches from beet tops. Place trimmed beets in a saucepan, cover with water and bring to a boil. Reduce heat to low and simmer until beets are tender, about 40 to 60 minutes; drain. When cool enough to handle, cut off the top end of beets and slip skins off with a paring knife. Chop beets roughly.

In a small nonstick skillet, heat oil over medium-low heat and sauté onion with caraway seeds until onion is translucent and caraway is fragrant. Transfer mixture to a food processor workbowl or blender container with beets and 2 cups of the water. Process mixture until smooth (in batches if using blender) and transfer pureed mixture to a bowl. To bowl, add remaining 1 cup water, lemon juice and salt and stir until blended. Chill well or heat through over low heat. Serve chilled or hot in shallow soup bowls topped with a dollop of sour cream.

# CURRIED PUMPKIN-MUSHROOM SOUP

*This easy recipe, prepared with canned pumpkin, makes a very satisfying winter supper entrée with hot bread or corn muffins and cole slaw.*

2 tbs. butter
⅔ cup finely chopped onion
½ lb. mushrooms, sliced
2 tsp. curry powder
2 tbs. all-purpose flour
3 cups *Vegetable Stock*, page 6 or
    purchased

1 cup water
1 cup whole milk
1 can (1 lb.) pumpkin
salt and pepper to taste
fresh cilantro leaves for garnish
lime wedges

In a large pot, melt butter over medium heat and sauté onion for 4 minutes. Stir in mushrooms and curry powder and sauté for 2 to 3 minutes. Add flour and sauté for 2 minutes. Stir in stock, water, milk and pumpkin and cook until heated through. Season with salt and pepper. Garnish each serving with cilantro and serve with lime wedges.

# BANANA SQUASH AND VEGETABLE SOUP

*This tasty, whole-meal soup goes well with cornbread, soda bread or muffins. Increase the amount of curry powder if you want a spicier soup.*

4 lb. banana squash
1 large russet potato (about ½ lb.)
6 cups water
2 tbs. butter
1 red or yellow bell pepper, seeded, ribs removed and finely chopped

1 large onion, finely chopped
2 tsp. curry powder, or more to taste
½ lb. spinach, well washed and chopped
salt to taste
lemon or lime wedges

Cut squash in half lengthwise, remove seeds and cut squash flesh into chunks; remove peelings from chunks. Peel potato and cut into chunks. Place squash and potato in a large pot with water and bring to a boil. Reduce heat to low and simmer, covered, for about 8 minutes, until squash is tender. In a nonstick skillet, melt butter over medium heat and sauté pepper and onion with curry powder for 4 to 5 minutes, or until softened. With a food processor or blender, puree squash-potato mixture in batches and return to pot. Stir in sautéed vegetables and spinach. Simmer for about 5 minutes, until spinach is cooked, and season with salt. Serve with lemon wedges.

# CURRIED RED LENTIL, CARROT AND CITRUS SOUP

*Here is an excellent after-game soup for a crowd. It's a satisfying entrée when accompanied by hot French rolls and sliced cheeses.*

3 qt. water
5 cups red lentils, rinsed
4 cups shredded carrots
6 cups *Vegetable Stock*,
   page 6 or purchased
3 tbs. olive oil
2 cups finely chopped onions
4 large cloves garlic, minced
2 tbs. curry powder
1 tsp. ground cumin
2 tsp. grated fresh ginger
¼ cup fresh lime juice
1 cup fresh orange juice
1-2 tsp. salt, or to taste
fresh cilantro leaves for garnish

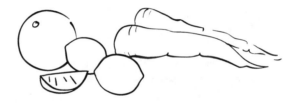

In a large pot, bring water to a boil and add lentils and carrots. Cook for 15 minutes, stirring frequently. Reduce heat to low, and simmer, covered, for 15 minutes. Add stock and continue to simmer, covered.

While mixture simmers, heat oil in a large nonstick skillet over medium heat and sauté onions for 5 minutes. Add garlic, curry and cumin to skillet and sauté for 4 to 5 minutes, until onions are tender and spices are fragrant. Add onion mixture and ginger to pot with lentils and simmer for about 30 minutes, until lentils are tender. Stir in lime juice, orange juice and salt and heat through. Serve garnished with cilantro leaves.

# CURRIED LENTIL AND EGGPLANT SOUP

*The curry powder can be added in increments, according to your taste. This makes a solid one-dish meal with hot bread and, if you wish, a light green salad.*

2 cups lentils, rinsed
7 cups water
4 cups *Vegetable Stock*, page 6 or purchased
3 tbs. olive oil
1½ cups chopped onions
1 stalk celery, sliced
1 tart green apple, peeled, cored and coarsely grated
about ¾ lb. eggplant, unpeeled, cut into ½-inch cubes
4 tsp. curry powder, or to taste
1½ tsp. grated fresh ginger
¼ tsp. cinnamon
¼ tsp. nutmeg
1 tsp. coarsely ground pepper
⅓ cup fresh lemon juice
1-2 tsp. salt, or to taste
dash cayenne pepper

In a large pot, bring lentils, water and 3 cups of the stock to a boil. Reduce heat to low and simmer, covered, for 30 minutes, or until lentils are tender, but still retain their shape.

In a nonstick skillet, heat 1 tbs. of the oil over medium heat and sauté onions and celery for 4 minutes. Add remaining 2 tbs. oil, apple, eggplant, curry, ginger, cinnamon, nutmeg and pepper and sauté for 8 minutes. Add remaining 1 cup stock, cover and simmer for about 20 minutes, until eggplant is tender. Transfer eggplant mixture to pot with lentils, add lemon juice and season with salt and cayenne. Serve in bowls.

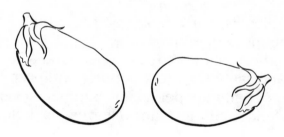

# LENTIL SOUP WITH CUMIN AND BARLEY

*Make a full meal from this good winter soup with hot whole grain bread or rolls.*

2 cups lentils, rinsed
½ cup unhulled barley or pearl barley
6 cups water
2 tbs. olive oil
1 cup finely chopped onion
3 large cloves garlic, minced
1 tbs. ground cumin

2 cups *Vegetable Stock*, page 6 or
  purchased
1-2 tsp. salt
⅓-½ cup red wine vinegar
freshly ground pepper to taste
red pepper flakes to taste
⅔ cup fresh cilantro leaves

In a large pot, bring lentils, barley and water to a boil. Reduce heat to low and simmer, covered, for about 1 hour.

In a nonstick skillet, heat oil over medium heat and sauté onion for 4 minutes. Add garlic and cumin and sauté for 3 to 4 minutes. Transfer mixture to pot and add stock, salt, vinegar, pepper and pepper flakes. Simmer, covered, for about 20 minutes, or until barley is tender. Stir in cilantro leaves just before serving.

# RUSSIAN POTATO AND CABBAGE BORSCHT

*Serve this filling soup with coarse dark bread and sharp cheese.*

3 cups sliced russet potatoes
1 large carrot, sliced
3 cups water
2 tbs. butter
1 large onion, halved and sliced
1 tsp. caraway seeds

4 cups chopped green cabbage
3 cups *Vegetable Stock*, page 6 or
    purchased
1 tsp. dill weed
salt and freshly ground pepper to taste
sour cream for garnish

In a large saucepan, bring potatoes, carrot and water to a boil. Reduce heat to low and simmer, covered, until vegetables are just tender; remove from heat and set aside. In a large pot, melt butter over medium heat and sauté onion for 3 minutes. Add caraway seeds and sauté for 2 minutes. Add cabbage and sauté briefly. Transfer potato-carrot mixture to pot and bring back to a simmer. Add stock and dill weed and simmer for 5 minutes. Season with salt and pepper. Serve in deep bowls with a dollop of sour cream.

# LEEK AND POTATO SOUP

*Serve this as an entrée with hot bread or biscuits, followed by a green salad.*

3 tbs. butter
4 large leeks, white part only, well washed,
    trimmed and thinly sliced
1½ lb. russet potatoes, peeled and
    thinly sliced
1½ cups *Vegetable Stock*, page 6
    or purchased
2 cups water
2 cups whole milk
salt and white pepper to taste
snipped fresh chives for garnish

   In a large pot, melt butter over low heat and sauté leeks until very tender; do not allow to brown. Add potatoes, stock and water and bring to a boil. Reduce heat to low and simmer, covered, until potatoes are tender. Stir in milk, but do not allow to boil. Season with salt and pepper and serve garnished with chives.

# POTATO AND LIMA BEAN CHOWDER

*This makes a particularly nice winter evening meal with cornbread or muffins.*

2 tbs. butter
1 medium onion, finely chopped
1 tsp. dill weed
3 cups diced peeled russet potatoes
2 cups diced carrots
4 cups *Vegetable Stock*, page 6 or purchased
2 cups water
1 pkg. (10 oz.) frozen lima beans
1 cup whole milk
salt and white pepper to taste
fresh parsley leaves for garnish

In a large pot, melt butter over medium heat and sauté onion for 4 minutes; add dill and sauté for 1 minute. Add potatoes, carrots, stock and water and bring to a boil. Reduce heat to low and simmer, covered, until vegetables are tender, but not mushy. Add lima beans and cook briefly. Stir in milk, but do not allow to boil. Season with salt and pepper and serve garnished with parsley.

# POTATO-CHEESE SOUP

*Here's a quickie lunch or light supper soup that goes well with whole grain bread and, perhaps, a little cole slaw.*

2 tbs. butter
1 large white onion, halved and thinly sliced
2 tsp. caraway seeds
1½ lb. russet potatoes, peeled and thinly sliced
2 cups water

2 cups *Vegetable Stock*, page 6 or purchased
2 cups whole milk
salt and white pepper to taste
1½ cups shredded Gruyère cheese or domestic Swiss cheese
minced fresh parsley for garnish

In a large pot, melt butter over medium heat and sauté onion for 4 minutes; add caraway seeds and sauté for 1 minute; do not allow onion to brown. Add potatoes, water and stock and bring to a boil. Reduce heat to low and simmer, covered, for about 8 to 10 minutes, until potatoes are tender. In batches, puree soup with a food processor or blender until smooth and return to pot with milk. Cook soup until heated through and season with salt and pepper. Serve hot with a generous scattering of cheese; garnish with parsley.

# ITALIAN BROCCOLI SOUP

*This works as a lunch entrée or a light supper with hot crusty bread and a salad.*

2 tbs. olive oil
3 tbs. chopped garlic
¼ cup uncooked white rice
2 lb. broccoli, trimmed and finely chopped
5 cups *Vegetable Stock*, page 6 or purchased, or use half water
salt and freshly ground pepper to taste
⅔ cup grated Parmesan or Asiago cheese

In a large pot, heat oil over medium heat and sauté garlic until slightly golden. Add rice and sauté until slightly dry. Add broccoli and stock and bring to a boil. Reduce heat to low and simmer, covered, for about 12 minutes, until broccoli and rice are tender. Remove 1 cup of the soup solids and puree with a food processor or blender. Return pureed mixture to pot and season soup with salt and pepper. Serve in shallow bowls and sprinkle with cheese.

# FRESH TOMATO SOUP
# WITH CILANTRO SAUCE

*A nice lunch soup when tomatoes are in season, this also makes a lovely first course.*

3 tbs. olive oil
1 cup chopped onion
1 tbs. minced garlic
2 cups *Vegetable Stock*, page 6 or purchased
about 4 cups peeled, seeded, chopped ripe tomatoes
salt to taste
*Cilantro Sauce*, follows

In a large pot, heat oil over medium heat and sauté onion for 4 minutes. Add garlic and sauté until vegetables are soft and golden, about 4 minutes. Add stock and tomatoes and bring to a boil. Reduce heat to low and simmer, covered, for 20 minutes. With a food processor or blender, carefully process soup until lightly blended and return to pot. Season with salt and cook until heated through. Serve in bowls with a dollop of *Cilantro Sauce*.

## CILANTRO SAUCE

2 tbs. olive oil
2 tbs. minced garlic
2 cups fresh cilantro leaves
¼ cup lime juice
1 jalapeño chile, stemmed and seeded
salt to taste

In a small saucepan, heat olive oil over medium heat and sauté garlic until golden. Transfer garlic to a blender container with cilantro leaves, lime juice and jalapeño and blend well. Transfer mixture to a bowl and season with salt.

# GAZPACHO

*Gazpacho, the famous soup from Spain, has many variations. Here are two different styles. **Classic Gazpacho** forms a nice summer meal with melted cheese sandwiches and a green salad. Serve **Quick Gazpacho** with quesadillas on whole wheat tortillas accompanied by a fruit salad.*

## CLASSIC GAZPACHO WITH AVOCADO

6 hard-cooked eggs
1/4 cup olive oil
3 cloves garlic, mashed
2 tsp. dry mustard
1/4 tsp. cayenne pepper
1/2 cup lime juice
4 cups *Vegetable Stock*, page 6 or
    purchased

4 cups tomato juice
5 medium-sized ripe tomatoes, cored,
    peeled, seeded and finely chopped
2 cups minced green bell peppers
1 large cucumber, peeled, seeded and
    finely chopped
salt to taste
3 Hass avocados

Separate egg yolks from whites; reserve whites for another use. With a fork, mash yolks with oil, garlic, mustard, cayenne and lime juice until smooth. Place stock and tomato juice in a large bowl and stir in yolk mixture. Stir in tomatoes, peppers, cucumber and salt. Refrigerate until well chilled. Serve garnished with peeled, sliced avocados.

## QUICK GAZPACHO

4 large ripe tomatoes, cored, peeled, seeded and finely chopped
3 cups V-8 juice
½ cup dry red wine
2 tbs. olive oil
1 tbs. red wine vinegar (do not substitute balsamic)
½ cup finely chopped green bell pepper
½ cup finely chopped sweet red onion
1 small cucumber, peeled, seeded and finely chopped
3 tbs. minced fresh cilantro
½ tsp. dried oregano
salt and cayenne pepper to taste

In a large bowl, combine tomatoes, V-8 juice, red wine, olive oil and vinegar; mix well. Stir in green pepper, onion, cucumber, cilantro and oregano. Season with salt and refrigerate until well chilled.

# CURRIED CAULIFLOWER SOUP

*Here is a nice first-course soup, served hot in the winter or chilled in the summer.*

7 cups trimmed, chopped cauliflower
3½ cups *Vegetable Stock*, page 6 or purchased, or use part water
2 tsp. canola or safflower oil
1 cup chopped onion
1½ tsp. curry powder
⅔ cup buttermilk
salt and white pepper to taste
fresh cilantro leaves for garnish

In a large pot, bring cauliflower and stock to a boil. Reduce heat to low and simmer, covered, until cauliflower is tender, about 8 minutes. In a small nonstick skillet, heat oil over medium heat and sauté onion for 4 minutes. Stir in curry powder and sauté for 1 minute. Transfer cauliflower mixture to a food processor workbowl or blender container with cooked onion; process until just slightly coarse in texture. Return mixture to pot and add buttermilk. If serving hot, heat through, but do not allow to boil; season with salt and pepper. If serving cold, season soup with salt and pepper, cool to room temperature and refrigerate until well chilled. Serve garnished with cilantro.

# CREAMY CABBAGE SOUP
# WITH BLUE CHEESE

*Complement this substantial soup with an equally substantial bread. Season the soup sparingly with salt due to the saltiness of the blue cheese.*

1 tbs. butter
1 medium onion, quartered and thinly
   sliced
½ tsp. dried thyme leaves
½ medium head green cabbage,
   shredded
½ cup water

2 cups *Vegetable Stock*, page 6 or
   purchased
½ cup sour cream
½ cup buttermilk
salt and freshly ground pepper to taste
2 oz. blue cheese, crumbled

In a large pot, melt butter over medium heat and sauté onion for about 5 minutes, until well softened. Add thyme and cabbage and sauté until cabbage begins to soften. Add water and stock and bring to a boil. Reduce heat to low and simmer, covered, for about 10 minutes, until cabbage is tender. Mix sour cream with buttermilk until blended. Remove soup from heat and slowly add sour cream mixture. Return soup to heat and gently cook until heated through, but do not allow to boil. Season with salt and pepper. Serve sprinkled with blue cheese.

# ZUCCHINI SOUP WITH CUMIN AND CINNAMON

*This low-fat soup is a good way to use up your zucchini crop at the end of the season. Try it as a lunch soup with French bread and cheese.*

1 lb. zucchini, sliced
2 cups *Vegetable Stock*, page 6 or
    purchased
2 tsp. canola oil
2/3 cup chopped onion

1/2 tsp. cinnamon
1/2 tsp. ground cumin
2/3 cup buttermilk
salt and white pepper to taste
fresh cilantro leaves for garnish

In a large pot, bring zucchini and stock to a boil. Reduce heat to low and simmer, covered, for about 6 minutes, until zucchini is tender. In a small nonstick skillet, heat oil over medium heat and sauté onion for 4 minutes. Add cinnamon and cumin and sauté for 1 minute. Transfer onion mixture to a food processor workbowl or blender container with zucchini mixture and process until blended; do not strain. Return mixture to pot, add buttermilk and gently cook until heated through, but do not allow to boil. Season with salt and pepper. Serve garnished with cilantro leaves.

# EGGS AND DAIRY

# EGGS AND DAIRY IN A VEGETARIAN DIET

Since its founding, the United States had been a culture dependent on eggs and dairy products. Over the years, this has changed somewhat with the influx of immigrants from Asian countries, for whom dairy products are not a major part of the diet. Still, many Americans prefer these excellent protein sources. When cooking vegetarian-style, one can find many creative ways to use eggs and dairy products.

The following recipes vary in ingredients and styles, but all of them feature eggs, milk products or cheese. Feel free to make your own substitutions according to your tastes and dietary requirements. Consider using a local dairy for your milk supply and a local egg ranch, which allows the chickens to roam and scratch, as your source for eggs.

A few of the recipes in this section call for cheeses that are more common to other countries, though most of these cheeses are also domestically produced. The United States has become a very fine cheese-making country, and each state has its specialties. You may want to familiarize yourself with the cheeses that are special in your area and experiment with them. As with all dishes, the quality of the raw ingredients makes all the difference in the end result.

# TOMATO RAREBIT

*This old classic loves the company of a spinach salad for lunch or dinner.*

2 large ripe tomatoes, cored and cut into thirds
salt and freshly ground pepper to taste
2 tbs. butter
1 tbs. Dijon-style mustard
½ tsp. dry mustard
2 tsp. Worcestershire sauce
½ tsp. paprika
¼ tsp. salt
1 lb. sharp cheddar cheese, diced
½ cup flat beer
2 egg yolks
¼ cup evaporated milk
6 large slices whole grain bread, lightly toasted

Heat broiler. Place tomato slices on a broiler pan and season lightly with salt and pepper. Place tomatoes 3 inches from heat source and broil for 2 minutes on each side; remove pan from oven and cover with foil to keep tomatoes warm. In the top of a double boiler, melt butter over simmering water. Add Dijon mustard, dry mustard, Worcestershire, paprika, salt and cheese, stirring as cheese melts. Add beer and continue to stir until cheese is completely melted. In a bowl, beat egg yolks with milk and add to cheese mixture; heat, stirring, until thickened and remove from heat. Place one piece of toast on each of 6 plates, top each toast slice with a tomato slice and spoon cheese sauce over the top. Serve immediately.

# VEGETABLE TORTA

*You might see this type of recipe referred to as a Spanish omelet. This basic torta calls for potatoes, onions and eggs, but any seasonal vegetables or herbs can be incorporated. Grated Parmesan, crumbled feta or most any cheese can be used in place of Asiago. When tomatoes are in season, it's nice to add a cup or so, chopped, to your tortas. This type of dish is well complemented by a green salad with a lemony vinaigrette.*

1 large russet potato or 2 smaller red potatoes
salt
2 cups chopped Swiss chard, or 3 cups
    chopped spinach, well washed and spun dry
¼ cup olive oil
1 small onion, finely chopped
½ tsp. dried oregano leaves
½ medium-sized red bell pepper, seeded,
    ribs removed and coarsely chopped
salt and freshly ground pepper to taste
3 eggs, lightly beaten with 3 tbs. water
1 cup freshly grated Asiago cheese

Peel russet potato (do not peel red potatoes) and cut into ½-inch or smaller pieces. Place potatoes in a small saucepan, cover with cold water and bring to a boil. Reduce heat to low, sprinkle lightly with salt and simmer, covered, for about 4 minutes, until just tender, but not mushy; drain and set aside. Steam chard until just tender, or steam spinach briefly until wilted; set aside.

In a 12-inch nonstick skillet over medium heat, add oil and sauté onion, oregano and pepper for 4 minutes; remove from heat. Arrange onion mixture in pan evenly. Distribute potato and chard evenly over onion. Season lightly with salt and liberally with pepper. If desired, cover pan and let stand until needed.

When ready to serve, reheat vegetables briefly over low heat. Pour egg mixture over vegetables in skillet, tilting skillet to distribute eggs as evenly as possible. Sprinkle cheese over eggs and cover. Cook for just a few minutes, until eggs are set and cheese is melted; do not overcook. Cut into wedges and serve immediately.

# ZUCCHINI AND BRIE TORTA

Servings: 2-4

*This torta goes nicely with a green salad dressed with a sharp vinaigrette and fresh bread.*

1 medium russet potato, peeled and diced
salt
2 tbs. olive oil
1 cup chopped green onions
3 cups thinly sliced zucchini
½ tsp. dried oregano leaves, crumbled
½ tsp. dried basil, crumbled
salt and freshly ground pepper to taste
2 oz. Brie cheese, thinly sliced
3 eggs, lightly beaten with 3 tbs. water

In a saucepan, cover potato with cold water and bring to a boil. Reduce heat to low, sprinkle lightly with salt and simmer, covered, for about 4 minutes, until potatoes are just tender, but not mushy; drain and set aside.

In a 10- or 12-inch skillet, heat oil over medium heat and sauté onions for 3 minutes. Add zucchini, oregano and basil and sauté for about 3 minutes, until zucchini is crisp-tender. Remove skillet from heat and distribute potatoes over zucchini and onions. Sprinkle lightly with salt and liberally with pepper. Lay cheese slices evenly over vegetables. Reheat vegetables briefly over low heat. Pour egg mixture over ingredients, tilting skillet to distribute eggs as evenly as possible. Cover and cook over low heat until eggs are just set; do not overcook. Cut into wedges and serve immediately.

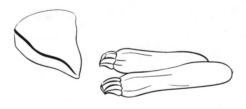

# SPINACH AND SUMMER SQUASH FRITTATA

*A frittata, Italian style, calls for several eggs and is cooked over a burner until it has a slightly crusty bottom and sides. It's not as light as an omelet or a torta. A frittata is easy to handle and is served hot or cold, cut into wedges. Like a torta, any combination of vegetables and cheese can be used for a frittata; often cheese is a minimal ingredient.*

1 lb. spinach, well washed and dried, coarsely chopped
¼ cup olive oil
1 lb. summer squash, such as zucchini or yellow crookneck squash, diced
2 large cloves garlic, minced
1 tsp. dried oregano leaves
½ tsp. dried basil
½ cup chopped fresh parsley
salt and freshly ground pepper to taste
8 eggs, lightly beaten with ¼ cup water
2 oz. Parmesan cheese, grated

Steam spinach until just wilted; set aside. In a 12-inch skillet with high sides, heat oil over medium heat and sauté squash, garlic, oregano and basil for about 3 minutes, until squash is crisp-tender. Reduce heat to low, stir in spinach and distribute evenly in pan. Sprinkle vegetables with parsley and season lightly with salt and pepper. Pour egg mixture over ingredients in skillet, tilting skillet to distribute eggs as evenly as possible. Cover pan and cook, checking frequently. When eggs begin to firm on the sides, pull them in slightly with a spatula and allow the center of eggs to flow to the outside. Sprinkle with Parmesan cheese, cover and continue to cook until eggs are set. Cut into wedges and serve hot or cooled.

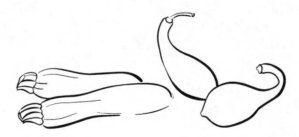

# POTATO AND STRING BEAN FRITTATA

*Serve this lunch, picnic or light supper entrée with a tomato salad and French bread. Substitute red potatoes for russets if desired.*

1 lb. russet potatoes, peeled and diced
salt
3 tbs. olive oil
1 cup finely chopped green onions
1 cup finely chopped red bell pepper
½ lb. string beans, cut into ½-inch pieces
1 tsp. dill weed
salt and freshly ground pepper to taste
8 eggs, lightly beaten with ¼ cup water
4 oz. Swiss cheese, shredded

Place potatoes in a small saucepan, cover with cold water and bring to a boil. Reduce heat to low, sprinkle lightly with salt and simmer, covered, until just tender, but not mushy; drain and set aside.

In a 12-inch skillet with high sides, heat oil over medium heat and sauté onions, pepper and string beans until string beans are crisp-tender. Add potatoes and distribute all vegetables evenly in skillet. Sprinkle vegetables with dill weed, salt and pepper. Pour egg mixture over vegetables, tilting skillet to distribute eggs as evenly as possible. Cover pan and cook, checking frequently. When eggs begin to firm on the sides, pull them in slightly with a spatula and allow the center of eggs to flow to the outside. Sprinkle eggs with cheese, cover and continue to cook until eggs are set. Cut into wedges and serve hot or cooled.

# VEGETARIAN MOUSSAKA

*Here is a new slant on a Middle Eastern classic. Serve it with a spinach salad and toasted pita bread.*

1 eggplant, about 1 lb., cut into ½-inch slices
salt
¼ cup olive oil
1 large onion, halved and thinly sliced
2 tbs. minced garlic
¼ cup butter
2 tbs. unbleached all-purpose flour
2 cups whole milk
2 cups shredded Monterey Jack cheese
red pepper flakes to taste
2 cups cooked white rice
1 cup chopped fresh flat-leaf parsley leaves
½ tsp. cinnamon
2 large ripe tomatoes, cored, peeled and thinly sliced
1 cup freshly grated Parmesan cheese

Heat oven to 375°. Sprinkle sliced eggplant with salt and let stand on paper towels for 30 minutes. Rinse eggplant, pat dry and place on a lightly oiled baking sheet. Brush eggplant slices with 2 tbs. of the oil and bake for 8 minutes.

In a nonstick skillet, heat remaining 2 tbs. oil over medium heat and sauté onion and garlic until softened; set aside. In a nonaluminum saucepan, melt butter over low heat, add flour and sauté for 1 minute. Slowly add milk and cook until heated through. Add cheese and cook, stirring, until thickened. Stir in pepper flakes and set aside.

In a bowl, mix rice, parsley and cinnamon with sautéed onion and garlic. Line the bottom of an 8-x-12-inch baking dish with ½ of the eggplant slices. Cover eggplant with tomato slices. Spread rice mixture evenly over tomatoes and cover with ½ of the cheese sauce. Top with remaining eggplant and remaining sauce and sprinkle with Parmesan cheese. Cover baking dish with aluminum foil and bake for 20 minutes. Remove foil and bake for about 6 to 8 minutes, until moussaka is hot, bubbly and lightly browned.

# CAULIFLOWER-CHEESE SOUFFLÉ

*Serve this with whole grain rolls and a mixed fruit or vegetable salad.*

2 cups chopped cauliflower
3 tbs. butter
1½ tbs. unbleached all-purpose flour
1½ cups warm milk
1 cup shredded Gruyère or domestic Swiss cheese
6 eggs, separated
½ tsp. dill weed
salt

Heat oven to 375°. Steam cauliflower until tender, cool slightly and chop finely; set aside. In a large nonaluminum saucepan, melt butter over low heat and stir in flour. Continue to cook for 1 minute, stirring constantly; add milk. With a wire whisk, beat mixture until very smooth and thickened. Add cheese and cook, stirring, until melted; remove from heat. Add egg yolks to cheese mixture and beat lightly. Stir in cauliflower, dill and salt. In a clean, oil-free bowl, beat egg whites until stiff peaks form and fold into cheese-cauliflower mixture. Carefully transfer mixture to a buttered 2-quart soufflé dish. Set dish in a pan of hot water and bake for 35 to 40 minutes, or until soufflé is puffed and center is set. Serve immediately.

# CORN, CHEESE AND CILANTRO SOUFFLÉ

Servings: 5

*Companion dishes to this soufflé could be a green salad and corn muffins.*

2 cups fresh, frozen or
  drained canned corn kernels
⅔ cup shredded sharp cheddar cheese
6 eggs, separated, plus 2 egg whites
¼ cup minced fresh cilantro
salt and freshly ground pepper to taste
¼ tsp. cream of tartar

Heat oven to 425°. In a large bowl, stir together corn, cheese, egg yolks and cilantro; season lightly with salt and pepper. In a clean, oil-free bowl, beat 8 egg whites until foamy. Add cream of tartar and beat until stiff peaks form. Carefully fold egg whites into corn mixture and gently transfer to a buttered 2-quart soufflé dish. Set dish in a pan of hot water and bake for 10 minutes; reduce oven heat to 375° and bake for 30 minutes, until soufflé is puffed and center is set. Serve immediately.

# FRESH TOMATO PIE

*Serve this preceded by a chilled soup and breadsticks.*

one 8- or 9-inch pie pastry, unbaked
1 cup shredded Monterey Jack cheese
4 large ripe tomatoes, cored and thinly sliced
2 eggs
⅔ cup milk
1 tsp. dried tarragon leaves
¼ tsp. salt
freshly ground pepper to taste
½ cup freshly grated Parmesan cheese

Heat oven to 350°. Line an 8- or 9-inch pie pan with pastry, prick pastry several times with a fork and sprinkle evenly with Jack cheese. Arrange ½ of the tomatoes evenly over cheese. In a bowl, whisk together eggs, milk, tarragon, salt and pepper. Pour ½ of the egg mixture evenly over tomatoes; top with remaining tomatoes and pour remaining egg mixture over the top. Sprinkle with Parmesan cheese and bake for 35 to 40 minutes, or until pastry is lightly browned and eggs are set at the center. Cut into wedges and serve immediately.

# SWEET ONION PIE

*Look for local sweet onions. The younger and flatter the onion, the sweeter it usually is. Try a tomato or green salad with this dish and your favorite country-style bread.*

3 tbs. canola or safflower oil
2 lb. sweet onions, thinly sliced
salt to taste
6 eggs
¼ cup minced fresh flat-leaf parsley
2 cups medium-fine soft French breadcrumbs
⅔ cup freshly grated Parmesan cheese

Heat oven to 350°. In a large, heavy-bottomed skillet, heat oil over low heat and sauté onions until very soft and golden, about 20 to 25 minutes. Season lightly with salt. Spread onion mixture evenly in a 10-inch pie pan. Whisk together eggs and parsley and pour evenly over onions. Mix breadcrumbs with Parmesan and sprinkle over eggs. Bake for 35 to 40 minutes, just until eggs are set at the center; take care not to overbake. Cut into wedges and serve immediately.

# SPINACH AND EGG PIE

*This makes a nice light supper or lunch entrée accompanied by a fruit salad. You can also cut the pie into thinner slices and serve it as an appetizer.*

one 8- or 9-inch pie pastry, unbaked
1 lb. fresh spinach, well washed
    and dried and coarsely chopped
4 eggs
1 cup sour cream
½ tsp. dill weed
1 cup soft French breadcrumbs
1 tbs. butter, melted
3 tbs. grated Parmesan cheese

Heat oven to 425°. Line an 8- or 9-inch pie pan with pastry and, with a fork, prick several times on the bottom and sides. Bake pastry for 8 minutes, or until very lightly browned. Remove pastry from oven and reduce oven heat to 350°. Briefly steam spinach, until just slightly wilted. Distribute spinach evenly over prepared pastry. In a bowl, beat eggs lightly with sour cream and dill and spread over spinach. Toss breadcrumbs with butter and cheese and sprinkle over eggs. Bake for 18 to 20 minutes, or until eggs are set at the center. Cut into wedges and serve immediately.

# POTATO AND CAULIFLOWER PIE

*Whip up extra mashed potatoes one evening and save them for this recipe. The pie makes a tasty supper with yellow vegetables and cole slaw.*

2 cups prepared mashed potatoes,
    warm or room temperature
2/3 cup unbleached all-purpose flour
3 tbs. soft butter
3/4 tsp. salt
1 head cauliflower, about 1 lb.

1 tbs. canola or safflower oil
1/2 cup chopped green onions
3 eggs
1 1/2 cups shredded Swiss cheese
1 tsp. dill weed
salt to taste

Heat oven to 350°. In a bowl, thoroughly mix potatoes, flour, butter and salt and press into the bottom and up the sides of a buttered 9-inch pie pan. Bake for 5 minutes; cool.

Trim cauliflower, break into small florets and steam for about 5 minutes, until tender, but not mushy; set aside. In a nonstick skillet, heat oil over medium heat and sauté onions until soft; remove from heat. In a bowl, beat eggs with 1 cup of the cheese, dill weed and salt. Stir in sautéed onions and cauliflower and transfer to pie shell. Sprinkle with remaining 1/2 cup cheese and bake for 20 minutes, or until eggs are set at the center. Cut into wedges and serve immediately.

# MUSHROOM QUICHE

*A quiche, always popular for lunch or dinner, can also be cut into thin slices and served as an appetizer. To make a meal of this recipe, serve it with steamed green or yellow vegetables and follow with a green salad, if desired.*

one single 8- or 9-inch pie pastry, unbaked
¾ cup milk
2 eggs, lightly beaten
½ tsp. salt
¼ tsp. nutmeg
freshly ground pepper to taste
2 tbs. butter
2½ cups sliced mushrooms
3 tbs. minced onion
1½ tbs. unbleached all-purpose flour
2 tbs. dry sherry
1 cup shredded Gruyère or domestic Swiss cheese

Heat oven to 425°. Line an 8- or 9-inch pie pan with pastry, prick pastry several times with a fork and bake for 5 minutes; remove from oven and cool to room temperature. Reduce oven heat to 350°. In a bowl, lightly whisk together milk, eggs, salt, nutmeg and pepper; set aside. In a 10- or 12-inch nonstick skillet, heat butter over medium-high heat and sauté mushrooms with onion until mushrooms begin to soften. Add flour and stir for 30 seconds. Remove skillet from heat and stir in sherry and milk-egg mixture. Transfer mixture to prepared pastry shell and sprinkle with cheese. Bake for 35 or 40 minutes, or until eggs are set at the center and pastry is slightly golden. Cut into wedges and serve immediately.

# POTATO AND EGG CURRY

Servings: 5

*East Indians love the combination of potatoes, eggs and curry. This easy recipe makes a complete meal served over rice. A condiment salad of chopped cucumbers in yogurt with fresh mint complements this menu nicely.*

2 lb. red potatoes, cut into bite-sized
   pieces
2 tbs. canola or safflower oil
1 small onion, chopped
2 large cloves garlic, minced
1 tbs. ground coriander
1 tsp. ground turmeric
1 tsp. ground cumin
1/2 tsp. salt
1/4 tsp. cayenne pepper
2 tbs. all-purpose flour

1/2 cup unsweetened coconut milk
1 1/2 cups *Vegetable Stock*, page 6 or
   purchased, or more if needed
2 tbs. lemon juice
1 1/2 cups frozen peas
5 hard-cooked eggs, each cut into
   eighths
1/4 cup fresh cilantro leaves
hot cooked rice
roasted peanuts for garnish
chutney

Place potatoes in a small saucepan, cover with cold water and bring to a boil. Reduce heat to low, sprinkle lightly with salt and simmer, covered, until just tender, but not mushy; drain and set aside.

In a 10- or 12-inch nonstick skillet, heat oil over medium heat and sauté onion and garlic for 4 minutes. Add coriander, turmeric, cumin, salt and cayenne and sauté until onion is soft and spices are fragrant. Sprinkle onion mixture with flour and sauté for 1 minute. Add coconut milk, stock and lemon juice and cook, stirring, until mixture is slightly thickened. Add peas and simmer briefly to soften. Stir in potatoes, eggs and cilantro and cook until heated through. If you desire a thinner mixture, stir in a small amount of stock. Serve over hot rice. Garnish with peanuts and pass chutney at the table.

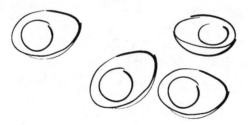

# POTATO-VEGETABLE SALAD WITH CREAMY LEMON DRESSING

*With a grilled cheese sandwich on whole grain bread, followed by sliced fresh fruit, this makes a very healthy lunch or light supper.*

¼ lb. red potatoes
½ lb. carrots, peeled
½ lb. cauliflower florets
½ lb. green beans
salt
*Creamy Lemon Dressing*, follows
1 medium cucumber

1 medium sweet onion, quartered and sliced
4 hard-cooked eggs, chopped
salt and pepper to taste
lemon juice, optional
½ cup chopped fresh cilantro leaves

Cut potatoes, carrots, cauliflower and beans into similar bite-sized pieces. Place potatoes and carrots in a saucepan, cover with cold water and sprinkle lightly with salt. Bring to a boil, reduce heat to low and simmer, covered, for 4 to 5 minutes, until potatoes are just tender, not mushy (carrots will still be slightly crisp); drain. Place potatoes and carrots in a bowl and, while still warm, toss lightly with a small amount of the dressing. Steam cauliflower and beans until crisp-tender and add to bowl, tossing well with a little more of the dressing. Place vegetable mixture in the refrigerator until cool.

To bowl, add cucumber, onion, eggs, salt and pepper and toss with a small amount of the dressing, if needed. Just before serving, taste salad and add more dressing or a small amount of lemon juice, if desired. Garnish servings with chopped cilantro.

**CREAMY LEMON DRESSING**
3/4 cup canola oil
2/3 cup fresh lemon juice
1/4 cup buttermilk
1/4 cup mayonnaise
2 tsp. dill weed
4 large cloves garlic, finely minced
2 tsp. coarsely ground pepper
1½ tsp. salt
1½ tsp. sugar

In a jar with a tight-fitting lid, combine oil, lemon juice, buttermilk, mayonnaise, dill, garlic, pepper, salt and sugar. Shake until well mixed.

# BAKED EGGS IN TOMATOES

*Here's a nice lunch or light supper recipe when tomatoes are in season. Look for large, firm, but ripe tomatoes for this recipe. A chilled soup and a green salad are good pals to this dish.*

4 large, ripe, nicely rounded tomatoes
1 tbs. olive oil
2 cloves garlic, minced
2 tbs. minced fresh flat-leaf parsley
salt and freshly ground pepper to taste
4 large eggs
2 tsp. butter
½ cup fine soft breadcrumbs
3 tbs. freshly grated Parmesan cheese

Heat oven to 400°. Slice stem end from tomatoes and carefully scoop out just the top half of the tomato pulp, leaving shell intact; reserve removed pulp. In a non-stick skillet, heat oil over medium-high heat and sauté tomatoes, cut-side up, for 2 minutes to soften slightly; carefully transfer tomatoes to a baking dish. Add garlic and parsley to skillet and sauté briefly; divide mixture among tomato cavities. Season cavities lightly with salt and pepper. Carefully break 1 egg into each tomato cavity. Wipe skillet clean and melt butter over medium heat; add breadcrumbs and sauté briefly. Top eggs with breadcrumbs and sprinkle with Parmesan cheese. Mix reserved tomato pulp with a small amount of water and pour in pan around tomatoes. Bake for 12 to 15 minutes, or until eggs are set. With a slotted spoon, transfer tomatoes to paper towels to drain briefly; place on serving plates and serve immediately.

# RATATOUILLE WITH POACHED EGGS

*A traditional French vegetable dish, ratatouille works very nicely as a vegetarian entrée topped with poached eggs and served with hearty bread.*

1 medium eggplant, about 1¼ lb., unpeeled and cut into 1-inch cubes
salt
3 tbs. olive oil
1 medium onion, coarsely chopped
1 tbs. minced garlic
1 large red bell pepper, seeded, ribs removed and cut into 1-inch pieces
2 medium zucchini, diced
1 tsp. dried oregano leaves
½ tsp. dried thyme leaves
½ tsp. dried basil
1 can (28 oz.) peeled plum tomatoes, drained and chopped, juice reserved
2 tbs. tomato paste
½ cup chopped fresh flat-leaf parsley
salt and red pepper flakes to taste
6 eggs
⅓ cup freshly grated Parmesan cheese

Place eggplant in a colander and sprinkle with salt. Let eggplant drain for 30 minutes; pat dry.

In a large nonstick skillet, heat 2 tbs. of the olive oil over medium heat and sauté eggplant slowly for 15 minutes. Add onion and sauté for 5 minutes. To skillet, add remaining 1 tbs. oil, garlic and pepper and sauté for 10 minutes. Add zucchini, oregano, thyme and basil and sauté for 5 minutes. Stir in tomatoes, tomato paste, parsley and reserved tomato juice. Season mixture lightly with salt and red pepper flakes, stir well and simmer, covered, for 25 minutes. Vegetables should be well cooked and soft. Taste for salt. If desired, cover ratatouille and set aside until ready to serve.

When ready to serve, reheat ratatouille, if needed. Make 6 small wells in hot ratatouille and carefully crack 1 egg into each well. Cover pan and cook until eggs are set. Serve portions in shallow bowls and sprinkle with cheese.

# MULTI-VEGETABLE RAGOUT
# WITH POACHED EGGS

*This is a wonderful dish for vegetable lovers, or for home gardeners looking for a way to use their bounty. Poached eggs add a touch of elegance and protein.*

3 tbs. olive oil
1 large onion, coarsely chopped
1 tbs. minced garlic
1 tsp. dried oregano leaves, crumbled
1 tsp. dried basil leaves, crumbled
1 tsp. dried thyme leaves, crumbled
1/4 tsp. red pepper flakes
1 can (14 1/2 oz.) cut tomatoes with juice
3 cups diced unpeeled eggplant
1/2 lb. green beans, cut into 1-inch pieces

2 cups diced cauliflower
2 cups diced red potatoes
1 medium red bell pepper, seeded, ribs removed and cut into 1-inch pieces
1/2 cup fresh flat-leaf parsley leaves
1 cup *Vegetable Stock*, page 6 or purchased
1 bay leaf
2 cups diced zucchini
salt
5-6 eggs, poached

In a large, deep skillet, heat olive oil over medium heat. Add onion and sauté for 5 minutes. Add garlic, oregano, basil, thyme and red pepper flakes and sauté for 2 minutes. Add tomatoes, eggplant, beans, cauliflower, potatoes, red pepper, parsley, stock and bay leaf and bring to a boil. Reduce heat to low and simmer, covered, for 20 minutes. Stir in zucchini and cook, covered, for about 3 minutes, until all vegetables are tender. Season with salt.

Just before serving, remove cover from skillet, increase heat to high and cook until liquid is reduced and thickened. Serve vegetables in shallow bowls and top each portion with a poached egg.

# EASY EGGPLANT PARMESAN WITH FRESH OREGANO

*Accompany this dish with a rice salad or potato salad and French bread.*

1 large eggplant, about 2-2½ lb.
all-purpose flour
2 eggs
3 tbs. water
½ tsp. salt
2½ cups dry French breadcrumbs
4-6 tbs. olive oil
½ lb. Monterey Jack cheese, thinly sliced
1 can (8 oz.) tomato sauce
2 tbs. fresh oregano leaves, or 2 tsp. dried
⅔ cup freshly grated Parmesan cheese
⅛ tsp. red pepper flakes

Heat oven to 400°. Trim ends from eggplant and cut into ½-inch-thick slices. On a paper towel, sprinkle an ample amount of flour. In a shallow bowl, beat eggs with water and salt. On another paper towel, spread breadcrumbs. In a large deep-sided skillet, heat 2 tbs. of the oil over medium heat. Using enough eggplant slices to fit skillet in a single layer, coat both sides of eggplant in flour, followed by egg mixture and breadcrumbs. Place coated eggplant slices in skillet and cook until browned on both sides. Spray a baking sheet with nonstick cooking spray and lay coated eggplant on baking sheet. Repeat coating and cooking process with remaining eggplant, adding remaining oil as needed to prevent sticking. Lay Monterey Jack slices on top of eggplant slices, dividing evenly. Spread cheese with tomato sauce and sprinkle with oregano. Mix Parmesan cheese with red pepper flakes and sprinkle a small amount on top of each slice. Bake for 8 to 10 minutes, until cheese is melted and bubbly. Serve immediately.

# EGGPLANT-TOMATO PIE

*Try this pie with a rice and vegetable salad and hot whole grain bread.*

1½ lb. eggplant
¼ cup olive oil
1 tsp. salt
2 eggs, lightly beaten
½ cup fine dry breadcrumbs
½ cup finely chopped onion

½ tsp. dried oregano leaves
½ tsp. freshly ground pepper
2 medium tomatoes, cored and thinly
    sliced
1 cup finely crumbled feta cheese

Heat oven to 400°. Spray a baking sheet with nonstick cooking spray. Trim ends from eggplant, peel and cut into ½-inch slices. Lay slices on prepared baking sheet, brush with 1 to 2 tbs. of the olive oil and sprinkle lightly with salt. Cover baking sheet with foil and bake for about 10 minutes, or until eggplant is very soft. Remove eggplant from oven and reduce oven heat to 375°. Transfer eggplant to a bowl and mash with a large fork or potato masher. To bowl, add remaining 2 to 3 tbs. olive oil, eggs, breadcrumbs, onion, oregano and pepper. Spoon mixture into a 9-inch pie pan, top with tomato slices and sprinkle with feta cheese. Bake for 20 to 25 minutes, until lightly browned and puffy. Cut into wedges and serve immediately.

# ZUCCHINI PIZZA

*In this unique pizza, grated zucchini is transformed into a pizza "crust." It's a creative way to use your zucchini crop, and to fool the kids into eating their vegetables. These toppings are only a suggestion; create your own unique versions. Serve this sort of pizza with sautéed vegetables or a tossed green or fruit salad.*

3 cups grated zucchini
3 eggs, well beaten
1/3 cup unbleached all-purpose flour
1/2 cup freshly grated Parmesan cheese
1/4 tsp. salt
1/2 cup minced sweet red onion
1/2 cup minced Italian pickled peppers

1 can (2 1/4 oz.) sliced black olives, drained
1/2 tsp. dried oregano leaves
1/2 tsp. dried basil
2 large, ripe tomatoes, thinly sliced
2 cups shredded mozzarella cheese

Heat oven to 450°. Press excess liquid from zucchini and place in a bowl. To bowl, add eggs, flour, Parmesan cheese and salt and mix with a fork until blended. Spread mixture evenly in a greased 9-x-13-inch baking dish and bake for 8 minutes. Remove dish from oven and reduce oven heat to 350°. Sprinkle "crust" with onion, peppers, olives, oregano and basil. Arrange tomatoes on top and sprinkle with mozzarella cheese. Bake for about 20 minutes, or until bottom of pizza is set and top is bubbly and lightly browned. Cut into rectangles and serve immediately.

# STUFFED ZUCCHINI

*This makes a great summer supper with sliced tomatoes, fresh fruit and hot whole grain bread.*

4 medium zucchini, about 7 inches long
3 tbs. butter
¾ cup finely minced onion
1 tbs. minced garlic
salt
3 eggs, lightly beaten
½ cup crumbled feta cheese

¾ cup shredded Monterey Jack cheese
3 tbs. chopped black olives
2 tbs. chopped fresh flat-leaf parsley
½ tsp. dill weed
1½ tbs. all-purpose flour
freshly ground pepper to taste
paprika

Heat oven to 375°. Cut zucchini in half lengthwise. With a spoon, scoop out zucchini flesh, leaving a ⅛-inch-thick shell, including ends. In a small nonstick skillet, heat butter over medium heat. Add zucchini flesh, onion, garlic and a light sprinkling of salt and sauté until onion is soft. Transfer mixture to a bowl and mix with eggs, cheeses, olives, parsley, dill, flour and pepper. Use mixture to fill zucchini shells and sprinkle with paprika. Place filled zucchini in a large rimmed baking dish with a small amount of water. Bake for 20 to 25 minutes, or until filling is set.

# CRUSTLESS GREEK ZUCCHINI QUICHE

*Any summer-type salad goes well with this light entrée, as well as any type of hearth-baked bread.*

1½ lb. zucchini
salt
2 tbs. olive oil
½ cup minced sweet onion
1 tsp. dried oregano leaves

½ cup sliced kalamata or other
    Greek olives
1 cup crumbled feta cheese
6 eggs
½ tsp. coarsely ground black pepper

Heat oven to 350°. Coarsely grate zucchini into a bowl. Sprinkle zucchini lightly with salt, toss with a fork and set aside for 10 minutes. Drain zucchini and press free of liquid. In a small skillet, heat oil over medium heat and sauté onion until softened. In a bowl, toss prepared zucchini with sauteéd onion, oregano, olives and feta cheese. In another bowl, beat eggs lightly with pepper and fold into zucchini mixture. Spoon mixture into a buttered 9-inch pie pan and bake until center is set, about 20 to 30 minutes; do not overbake. Cut into wedges and serve immediately.

# MELTED CHEESE SANDWICHES
# WITH SAUTÉED VEGETABLES

*As a lunch, this is nice with sliced fresh fruit. For supper, you could add a light soup. This recipe is easy to double and it's simple enough for kids to make.*

1 tbs. olive oil
1 small sweet onion, thinly sliced
1 small bell pepper, any color, seeded,
    ribs removed and thinly sliced
1 cup sliced mushrooms
4 thick slices hearty whole grain bread
1 oz. Monterey Jack, cheddar or Swiss cheese, sliced
½ tsp. dried oregano leaves
freshly ground pepper to taste

In a nonstick skillet, heat oil over medium heat and sauté onion and bell pepper for 3 minutes. Add mushrooms and sauté until just softened. Remove skillet from heat and keep contents warm. Toast bread lightly. Arrange cheese slices on 2 slices of bread, place on a toaster-oven pan and toast just enough to melt cheese. Distribute vegetables over cheese, sprinkle with oregano and pepper and top with remaining toasted bread. Serve immediately.

# CHEESE-CARAWAY
# VEGETABLE POCKET SANDWICH

*Serve this sandwich for a luncheon, picnic or light supper with a bean salad. Look for caraway Jack cheese in a specialty food store or deli. If you can't find it, substitute your favorite type of flavored Jack cheese.*

2 cups shredded caraway Jack cheese
1½ cups finely shredded green cabbage
1 cup finely shredded carrot
¼ cup minced sweet onion or green onions
¼ cup nonfat plain yogurt
¼ cup mayonnaise
4 pita breads, warmed and halved crosswise
2 medium tomatoes, cored and thinly sliced

In a bowl, toss cheese, cabbage, carrot and onion with a fork until well mixed. In another bowl, stir together yogurt and mayonnaise and stir into cheese-cabbage mixture. Spoon mixture into the center of pita breads, dividing evenly, and place on serving plates. Arrange tomato slices on plates with each sandwich.

# QUESADILLAS

Makes 2

*This is the Mexican equivalent of the American grilled cheese sandwich. It is just as versatile, as all kinds of extras can be added to the finished quesadilla. Consider sautéed vegetables, sliced tomatoes, shredded lettuce or cabbage, salsas and various beans as accompaniments. Quesadillas are a wonderful compliment to soups, grain dishes and bean dishes. And, they're great for kids to make. A little oil is necessary when making quesadillas with corn tortillas, as the oil makes the tortillas flexible. However, using oil with flour tortillas is optional: it makes the outside of flour tortillas crispy.*

two 8-inch corn or flour tortillas
2 oz. sliced or shredded cheese, or more to taste
oil, optional

Lay 1 of the tortillas on a work surface and place a small amount of cheese on ½ of the tortilla, near the center. Heat a skillet over medium heat, and add a small amount of oil if desired. Place tortilla with cheese flat in skillet and heat until tortilla is warmed and/or flexible. Fold tortilla in half over cheese and cook, flipping occasionally, until cheese is melted and tortilla is lightly browned. Repeat process with remaining ingredients.

# GRAINS, NUTS AND SEEDS

# GRAINS, NUTS AND SEEDS
# IN A VEGETARIAN DIET

One of the wonderful aspects of the healthy food revolution has been the incorporation of more whole grains into our modern diet. It is interesting to note that in most of the world, grains provide about fifty percent of the dietary protein. Grains are rich in B vitamins, and lack only one essential amino acid (lysine) which can be provided by combining them with other protein-rich foods (see page 3).

America has been primarily a wheat-based culture, but thanks to the influx of people from areas of the world where rice is a staple, and the interest in healthful foods in the last decades of this century, we are now multi-grain in our taste. We have not only learned to appreciate the various types of Asian rices, but we have been introduced to the healthy brown rice that grows well here in our country. In addition, we have learned to regard cornmeal as a grain, and to add to our diet other grains, such as millet, buckwheat, rye, barley and, of course, bulgur wheat. There are other exotic grains on the market today that you may wish to try, too. Grains are here to stay, and we owe it to ourselves to accept their gifts of nutrients, fiber and texture to our diets, assuring us of longer, healthier lives.

# GLOSSARY OF GRAINS

*As a general rule, 1 cup uncooked grain yields about 3 cups when cooked. All grains taste better seasoned with a little salt, but the amount will depend on the saltiness of the cooking liquid.*

**BARLEY**: In the pearl form, barley is mild and starchy. In its unhulled form, barley has a nutty flavor and more texture. Barley is an excellent addition to casseroles, or can stand alone as a side dish. It is great in soups, such as *Lentil Soup with Cumin and Barley*, page 16. When cooking, use 1 part barley to 2 parts water or broth. Bring mixture to a boil, reduce heat to low and simmer, covered, for 35 to 45 minutes.

**RICE**: Brown rice is the unpolished rice grain that still has the bran intact. It has a nutty flavor and is available in short- or long-grain form. White rice has had the bran removed, or is "polished." It comes in both long-grain and short-grain varieties. Rice can be added to soups, stews, casseroles, salads, baked goods or side dishes. Use 1 part rice to 2 parts water or broth. Bring to a boil, reduce heat, and simmer, covered, for 18 to 20 minutes for white rice, or 30 to 40 minutes for brown rice.

**MILLET**: Millet is a very mild, delicate grain that is known to aid digestion. It's good in stuffings and casseroles, or with vegetable sauces. Use 1 part millet to 2½ parts water or broth. Bring mixture to a boil, reduce heat to low and simmer, covered, for 20 minutes.

**BULGUR WHEAT**: Bulgur refers to wheat kernels that have been toasted and cracked. It cooks quickly and has a light, nutty flavor. Bulgur is very good in stuffings, casseroles, baked goods and salads. Use 1 part bulgur to 1½ parts water or broth. Bring mixture to a boil, reduce heat to low and simmer, covered, for 12 to 15 minutes. It can also be soaked in boiling water for about 30 minutes. Drain well before using.

**CORN**: Corn is not a grain, strictly speaking, but in the form of hominy grits, cornmeal and polenta, it functions as one. It is a good protein complement, particularly as polenta and hominy grits. These products vary in cooking time; it's best to consult the cooking instructions on the packages.

**OTHER GRAINS**: There are many other delicious grains and grain-like plants that are useful in a vegetarian diet for their protein complements. Wheat berries, rye, triticale and buckwheat are just some of the examples.

# NUTS AND SEEDS

Nuts and seeds are high in B vitamins and minerals. They are also a good source of protein and fiber in a vegetarian diet and provide a rich texture and flavor to many dishes. They are, however, high in fat, so those who are watching fat calories should use them sparingly. Since their fat content makes them prone to rancidity, it is best to purchase nuts and seeds in small quantities and keep them in the refrigerator or freezer.

**ALMONDS**: A rich source of calcium, almonds are considered an alkaline food and can balance the many acidic foods in a vegetarian diet.

**PEANUTS**: Commonly grouped with nuts, peanuts are actually legumes. As legumes, peanuts are high in fat; but they are among the lowest in fat in the nut category.

**PECANS**: Particularly high in fat, pecans should be kept refrigerated or frozen to avoid rancidity. Their lovely rich flavor goes well in burger and loaf recipes.

**PINE NUTS**: Although high in protein, pine nuts are more perishable than most nuts and are best purchased in small quantities and stored in the freezer.

**SUNFLOWER KERNELS**: These are an excellent source of protein and potassium. They, too, should be stored in the refrigerator or freezer.

# STUFFED SWISS CHARD

*This is a new take on stuffed cabbage or stuffed grape leaves. It is a good dish to prepare during the summer, or when chard is growing abundantly and its leaves are large, but tender.*

16 large Swiss chard leaves (about
   1¼ lb.)
3 tbs. olive oil
1 cup finely chopped onion
2 large cloves garlic, minced
⅓ cup minced fresh flat-leaf parsley
1 tsp. dried oregano leaves, crumbled

2 cups chopped fresh mushrooms
2½ cups cooked brown or white rice
1 egg, lightly beaten
2 cups crumbled feta cheese
¼ cup minced kalamata or Greek
   green olives, optional
salt and freshly ground pepper to taste

**QUICK TOMATO SAUCE**
1 tbs. olive oil
1 small onion, thinly sliced
1 can (12 oz.) tomato juice

¼ cup minced fresh flat-leaf parsley
2 tsp. cinnamon

Wash chard leaves well and trim stalks at the base of leaves. Briefly steam chard until flexible enough to roll, in batches if necessary; set aside.

In a 12-inch nonstick skillet, heat oil over medium heat and sauté onion for 3 minutes. Add garlic, parsley and oregano, and sauté until onion is soft and garlic is golden. Add mushrooms and sauté until mushrooms are slightly softened, but not yet giving off liquid; transfer mixture to a large bowl. To bowl, add rice, egg, ½ cup of the feta, olives, salt and pepper and mix gently. Lay chard leaves flat on a work surface. Place about ¼ cup of the vegetable-rice mixture at one end of a chard leaf and roll up tightly, tucking in the sides. Set stuffed leaf seam-side down in a large pot. Repeat stuffing process with remaining chard leaves and rice mixture.

For sauce, heat oil in a skillet over medium heat and sauté onion for 6 minutes. Stir in tomato juice, parsley and cinnamon and simmer, uncovered, for 5 minutes. Pour sauce over stuffed chard leaves and cover pot. Cook over low heat for about 20 minutes, until heated through. Serve stuffed chard with sauce in shallow bowls and sprinkle with remaining 1½ cups feta cheese.

# MEXICAN RICE, BEAN AND CORN CASSEROLE

*This is a good way to use leftover rice, beans or corn. It's easy to assemble and is nice for a family or company meal. If serving children, choose a mild salsa. This dish can be made a few hours in advance and refrigerated. Let it stand at room temperature for at least 40 minutes before baking. A green salad is all that is necessary to round out the meal.*

3 tbs. canola, corn or safflower oil
⅔ cup finely chopped onion
1 cup finely chopped green bell pepper
2½ cups cooked rice
1½ cups cooked pinto, pink or
    kidney beans, rinsed and drained
2 cups shredded Monterey Jack cheese
½ cup fresh, frozen or drained canned
    corn
2 cups fresh or canned salsa

½ cup sour cream
1 can (2½ oz.) sliced ripe olives
½ cup chopped fresh cilantro
½ tsp. ground cumin
salt to taste
12 small corn tortillas
½ cup freshly grated Parmesan or
    Asiago cheese

Heat oven to 375°. In a large nonstick skillet, heat 1 tbs. of the oil over medium heat and sauté onion and pepper for about 8 to 10 minutes, until very soft. Transfer vegetables to a large bowl and add rice, beans, cheese, corn, 1 cup of the salsa, sour cream, olives, cilantro and cumin. Stir mixture with a large fork until well mixed and season with salt.

Heat 2 tsp. of the oil in a large skillet over medium-high heat, add 4 of the tortillas and cook until softened, about 1 minute. Cut heated tortillas in half and place in the bottom of a 9-x-13-inch baking dish or casserole. Spread tortillas with ⅓ cup of the salsa; top with ½ of the rice mixture. Repeat layering process.

Soften remaining 4 tortillas in remaining 2 tsp. oil according to method above. Cut heated tortillas in half and place on top of rice mixture. Cover with remaining ⅓ cup salsa. Sprinkle with Parmesan or Asiago cheese and cover tightly with foil. Bake for 35 minutes, or until very hot and bubbly.

# CURRIED BULGUR-STUFFED RED PEPPERS

Servings: 6

*Make this entrée into a hearty meal with a tomato salad and your favorite bread or muffins.*

1 cup bulgur wheat
2 cups boiling water
6 large red bell peppers
2 tbs. olive oil
⅔ cup finely chopped onion
2 large cloves garlic, minced
1½ cups finely chopped mushrooms
⅓ cup grated apple
1 tbs. curry powder, or more to taste
1 tsp. grated fresh ginger, or more to taste
½ tsp. ground cumin, or more to taste
salt and freshly ground pepper to taste
2 eggs, lightly beaten
1 cup crumbled feta cheese

Place bulgur in a bowl, cover with boiling water and let stand for 30 minutes; drain and press free of liquid.

Heat oven to 375°. Cut peppers in half lengthwise and remove seeds, ribs and end with core. Steam peppers for about 4 to 5 minutes, until crisp-tender; set aside. In a large skillet, heat oil over medium heat and sauté onion for 2 minutes. Stir in garlic, mushrooms, apple, curry, ginger and cumin and sauté until mixture is soft and blended. Transfer mixture to a bowl with prepared bulgur and mix well. Season with salt and pepper. Add eggs and mix well. Heap bulgur mixture into pepper cavities, dividing evenly, and top with feta cheese. Place peppers in a shallow baking dish with a small amount of water. Cover with foil and bake for 15 to 20 minutes, or until filling is set.

# VEGETABLE CURRY WITH RICE

*Serve this over hot cooked brown or white rice. With the condiments, this curry is a complete meal.*

2 medium red potatoes, diced
salt
2 tbs. butter
1 medium onion, coarsely chopped
2 large cloves garlic, minced
1 green bell pepper, seeded, ribs
   removed and coarsely chopped
1½ tbs. curry powder
2 tsp. grated fresh ginger
2 cups green bean pieces, ½-inch
   pieces
2 cups broccoli florets

½ cup chopped mushrooms
1½-2 cups cold *Vegetable Stock*, page
   6 or purchased
salt and red pepper flakes to taste
2 tsp. cornstarch, optional
hot cooked rice
raisins
peanuts
chutney
plain yogurt

80 GRAINS, NUTS AND SEEDS

In a saucepan, cover potatoes with cold water, sprinkle lightly with salt and bring to a boil. Reduce heat to low and simmer, covered, for about 5 minutes, until potatoes are tender, but not mushy; drain and set aside.

In a large nonstick skillet, melt butter over medium heat and sauté onion for 4 minutes. Add garlic and pepper and sauté for 2 minutes. Stir in curry and ginger and sauté for 2 minutes. Add beans, broccoli and mushrooms and sauté briefly. Add 2/3 cup of the stock. Reduce heat to low, cover and simmer just until vegetables are crisp-tender. Stir in potatoes and enough of the stock to make a slightly soupy mixture. Season with salt and red pepper flakes.

If you desire a thickened sauce, stir cornstarch into ½ cup of the cold stock and add to skillet. Heat gently, stirring, until thickened. Serve over rice and sprinkle with raisins and peanuts. Accompany servings with chutney and plain yogurt.

# RICE AND BEAN CASSEROLE

*This complete protein dish merely needs a green salad dressed with a lemon or lime vinaigrette to round out the meal.*

1 tbs. corn oil
1 small onion, finely chopped
1 large clove garlic, minced
3 cups cooked brown or white rice
1½ cups sour cream
1 cup corn kernels
1 cup drained canned pinto beans
1 can (4 oz.) chopped mild green chiles
½ can (2¼ oz. can) sliced ripe olives, drained
2 tbs. finely chopped fresh cilantro
2 cups shredded Monterey Jack cheese

Heat oven to 350°. In a small nonstick skillet, heat oil over medium heat and sauté onion and garlic for 5 minutes. Transfer onion mixture to a bowl with rice and sour cream; mix well. In another bowl, mix corn, beans, chiles, olives and cilantro. Lightly coat a 1½-quart casserole with nonstick cooking spray. Spread ½ of the rice mixture in prepared casserole. Top rice with corn-bean mixture and sprinkle with 1 cup of the cheese. Spread remaining rice mixture over cheese and sprinkle with remaining 1 cup cheese. Bake, covered, for 25 minutes. Increase oven heat to 400°, uncover and bake until cheese browns and becomes slightly crusty, about 5 minutes.

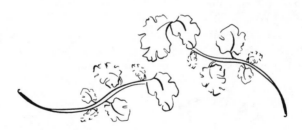

# RICE AND BEAN TACOS
# WITH FRESH TOMATO SALSA

*This is a good kids meal and they can actually do all the preparation. Serve these tacos with a fruit salad, perhaps made with papaya and orange. Be careful when working with chiles; wash your hands well afterward. If you prefer, you can heat the tortillas in foil in a 350° oven for 15 minutes. However, tortillas cooked on the burner get little dark spots and an authentic flavor.*

1 tbs. corn oil
1 small onion, finely chopped
2 cups cooked brown or white rice
1 can (15 oz.) kidney beans, drained
1 cup finely chopped fresh tomatoes
    or drained canned tomatoes
salt to taste
2 cups shredded Monterey Jack cheese
*Fresh Tomato Salsa*, follows
2 cups finely shredded green cabbage
12 corn tortillas

In a large nonstick skillet, heat oil over medium heat and sauté onion until softened. Stir in rice, beans and tomatoes and sauté until mixture is heated through. Stir in salt, remove from heat and keep warm.

When ready to eat, place bowls of cheese, salsa and cabbage on the table. Heat tortillas directly on a hot electric burner, gas burner or griddle, flipping back and forth until warm and flexible. Fill each prepared tortilla with a generous amount of rice-bean filling. Let diners add cheese, salsa and cabbage to their tacos at the table.

## FRESH TOMATO SALSA
2 large, very ripe tomatoes, peeled, cored, seeded and chopped
2/3 cup finely chopped onion
1-2 fresh serrano chiles, seeded and minced
3 tbs. finely chopped fresh cilantro
salt to taste
fresh lime juice to taste

In a glass bowl, mix tomatoes, onion, chiles and cilantro. Stir in salt and lime juice and let stand for 20 minutes to blend flavors.

# GARLICKY CHEESE GRITS

*Everyone seems to love this dish, and it makes a good entrée with steamed vegetables and a green salad or cole slaw. This recipe doubles nicely, but it will take a few minutes longer to cook.*

3 cups water
1 cup grits
½ tsp. salt
2 tbs. butter
3 cups shredded sharp cheddar cheese

¼ cup milk
2 large cloves garlic, minced
3 eggs, lightly beaten
cayenne pepper to taste
paprika

Heat oven to 375°. In a 2-quart saucepan, bring water to a boil. Slowly pour in grits, stirring constantly. Stir in salt and cook over medium heat for about 5 minutes, until mixture is thickened. Stir in butter, 2 cups of the cheese, milk and garlic and cook, stirring, until cheese is melted. Remove mixture from heat and fold in eggs and cayenne. Pour mixture into a buttered 1½-quart casserole or soufflé dish. Sprinkle with remaining 1 cup cheese and a small amount of paprika. Bake for 50 minutes, or until dish puffs up and center is set.

# BASIC POLENTA

*Polenta can serve as a base for many vegetarian recipes, such as **Cheesy Polenta Casserole**, page 88. Polenta thickens quickly, but it must cook long enough for the grains to soften. The texture of polenta grains seems to vary, as will the cooking time. Taste the polenta to determine its doneness: it should be creamy and not too grainy in the mouth. If it's not quite done, add a bit more liquid.*

4 cups water, or more if needed
1 tsp. salt
1 cup polenta

2 tbs. butter, optional
1/3 cup freshly grated Parmesan cheese, optional

In a saucepan, bring water and salt to a boil. Slowly add polenta, stirring constantly, and cook over medium-low heat for about 30 minutes, until thickened and smooth. Add more water if mixture becomes too thick. If desired, stir in butter and Parmesan.

Pour cooked polenta into an oiled bowl or casserole and use as desired. Or, pour polenta into an oiled loaf pan and refrigerate until cool and firm. Remove polenta from pan and cut into slices for grilling or frying.

# CHEESY POLENTA CASSEROLE

*Today, tasty prepared polenta can be found in a roll in most supermarket delis. You can use it instead of **Basic Polenta** in this recipe to save time. Take care not to overcook purchased polenta, as it can become very soft. Serve this dish with a green salad and hot bread.*

3 tbs. olive oil
1½ cups chopped onion
2 small Japanese eggplants, about
    ½ lb., unpeeled, sliced
3 large cloves garlic, minced
½ tsp. fennel seeds
1 large red bell pepper, seeded, ribs
    removed and coarsely chopped
1 tsp. dried oregano leaves
½ tsp. dried thyme leaves

½ tsp. dried basil leaves
2½-3 lb. fresh tomatoes, cored, peeled,
    seeded and chopped
salt and pepper to taste
1 double-batch *Basic Polenta*, page 87,
    or 2-2½ lb. purchased prepared
    polenta
1 pt. ricotta cheese
3 cups shredded mozzarella cheese
⅔ cup freshly grated Parmesan cheese

In a nonstick skillet, heat oil over medium heat and sauté onion for 3 minutes. Add eggplants, garlic and fennel seeds and sauté for 5 to 6 minutes. Add bell pepper, oregano, thyme and basil and sauté for about 4 to 6 minutes, until vegetables are softened. Stir in tomatoes and cook for 4 minutes. Season with salt and pepper and set aside.

Pour ½ of the polenta into a lightly oiled 12-inch ovenproof skillet with high sides, or into an equivalent-sized baking dish. Spread ricotta cheese over polenta. Sprinkle ricotta with 2 cups of the mozzarella cheese. Top mozzarella with ⅓ of the vegetable mixture. Top vegetable mixture with remaining polenta, using a knife to smooth evenly. Top polenta with remaining vegetable mixture and sprinkle with remaining 1 cup mozzarella cheese and Parmesan cheese. Cover skillet tightly with foil, set aside for up to 2 hours or bake immediately.

When ready to bake, heat oven to 450°. Bake casserole for 20 minutes, or until hot and bubbly and slightly browned on top. Cut into wedges to serve.

**NOTE**: When using purchased polenta in rolls, slice rolls into ¾-inch rounds. Layer rounds with remaining ingredients according to directions.

# MILLET PATTIES

*These delicate patties are nice topped with sautéed mushrooms. Serve them with a hot soup in the winter. In the summer, a nice compliment is **Greens, Nut and Cheese Salad**, page 94.*

1 tbs. canola oil, plus more for frying
1 cup uncooked millet
2½ cups water
1 tbs. olive oil
⅔ cup finely chopped sweet onion
½ cup minced red bell pepper
½ lb. young Swiss chard, well
    washed and finely chopped
½ tsp. ground cumin
⅔ cup finely chopped almonds
salt to taste
⅓ cup unbleached all-purpose flour

In a heavy-bottomed saucepan, heat 1 tbs. canola oil over medium heat. Add millet and sauté for 2 to 3 minutes, until dry and nutty in fragrance. Add water and bring to a boil. Reduce heat to low and simmer, covered, for 18 to 20 minutes, until millet is fluffy and liquid is absorbed.

In a nonstick skillet, heat olive oil over medium heat and sauté onion and pepper for 3 minutes. Stir in chard and sauté for about 5 to 6 minutes, until chard is softened. Transfer cooked millet to a bowl with cooked vegetables, cumin, almonds, salt and flour and mix well. Shape millet mixture into 6 patties, place on a plate and let stand to firm slightly.

In a nonstick skillet, heat a small amount of canola oil over medium heat. Fry patties until nicely browned on both sides and heated through.

# SOUTH-OF-THE-BORDER BURGERS

*Appealing to kids, these can be shaped into narrow patties and rolled in flour tortillas with **Fresh Tomato Salsa**, page 85. Or, sandwich round patties between bun halves and make them into burgers with the works. Cole slaw is an appropriate accompaniment.*

2½ cups cooked brown rice
2 cups cooked and drained pinto beans
1 cup finely chopped red bell pepper
⅔ cup corn kernels
½ cup finely chopped sweet onion
2 large cloves garlic, minced

¼ cup finely chopped fresh cilantro
2 tsp. ground cumin
salt to taste
½-¾ cup fine dry breadcrumbs
¼ cup canola or corn oil
8 flour tortillas or sandwich buns

With a food processor, process rice and beans until coarsely ground and even in texture. Transfer mixture to a bowl with bell pepper, corn, onion, garlic, cilantro and cumin and mix well. Mix in salt and enough breadcrumbs to hold a shape. Form mixture into 8 firm patties, either cigar- or burger-shaped.

In a large nonstick skillet, heat oil over medium-high heat. Cook patties, 4 at a time, for about 3 minutes on each side. Repeat with remaining patties. Serve in flour tortillas or buns.

# RICE, PEANUT AND VEGETABLE SALAD

*This makes a good lunch entrée with fresh bread and fruit. Or, serve it with soup and bread for supper. For best results, make the rice and cool it just before making the salad.*

4 cups cooked white or brown rice,
   cooled
1 cup dry-roasted peanuts
2/3 cup cooked peas, cooled
2/3 cup cooked corn kernels
2/3 cup minced sweet onion
2/3 cup minced red bell pepper
1/2 cup chopped fresh flat-leaf parsley

1/2 cup olive oil
1/4 cup red wine vinegar
2 tsp. Dijon-style mustard
1 tsp. dried oregano leaves
1 tsp. sugar
1/2 tsp. freshly ground pepper
salt to taste

In a bowl, combine rice, peanuts, peas, corn, onion, bell pepper and parsley; mix well. In another bowl, whisk together olive oil, vinegar, mustard, oregano, sugar, pepper and salt until blended. Add a small amount of dressing to rice mixture and toss until ingredients are well coated. Just before serving, toss salad with more dressing, if desired.

# GREENS, NUTS AND CHEESE SALAD

*For lunch, accompany this with fresh fruit and bread. For dinner, add a soup.*

5 cups torn romaine lettuce leaves
1 small bunch watercress
1 small sweet red onion, thinly sliced
1 large carrot, cut into thin 2-inch strips
1 cup pecan halves
⅓ lb. Swiss cheese, cut into thin 2-inch strips
*Creamy Lemon Dressing*, page 53, to taste

In a salad bowl, combine lettuce, watercress, onion, carrot, pecans and cheese and toss well. When ready to serve, toss with *Creamy Lemon Dressing* until ingredients are well coated.

# CRUNCHY VEGETABLE-RICE SALAD

*For a luncheon, offer fresh fruit and rolls as complements to this salad. For supper, offer soup and freshly baked bread.*

3 cups cooked brown or white rice, cooled
1 cup coarsely chopped walnuts
1 cup chopped peeled cucumber
⅔ cup finely chopped green onions
⅔ cup finely chopped red bell pepper
⅔ cup cooked, cooled, fresh or frozen peas
⅓ cup sunflower kernels, toasted

⅓ cup olive oil
⅓ cup canola oil
⅓ cup tarragon-flavored white wine vinegar
1 tsp. sugar
1 tsp. coarsely ground pepper
½ tsp. Dijon-style mustard
½ tsp. salt

In a salad bowl, combine rice, walnuts, cucumber, green onions, bell pepper, peas and sunflower kernels and toss well. In another bowl, whisk together oils, vinegar, sugar, pepper, mustard and salt until blended; taste for seasoning. Add a small amount of dressing to salad bowl and toss until ingredients are well coated. Just before serving, toss salad with more dressing, if desired.

# BROWN RICE AND PINE NUT PILAF

*To make a complete meal, pilafs can be served as companion dishes to soups, salads or sandwiches. Cooking pilafs in the oven makes them fluffier and less likely to stick than when cooked on the stovetop.*

3 tbs. butter
1 cup finely chopped onion
1 cup shredded carrots, pressed free of liquid
1 cup long-grain brown rice
2⅓ cups *Vegetable Stock*, page 6 or purchased
salt to taste
⅓ cup finely minced fresh flat-leaf parsley
⅓ cup pine nuts, toasted

Heat oven to 350°. In a 2-quart, heavy-bottomed ovenproof saucepan, melt butter over medium heat and sauté onion and carrots for 4 minutes. Stir in rice and sauté until rice grains are dry and slightly golden. Add stock, bring to a boil and season lightly with salt. Cover pan, place in oven and bake for 30 minutes, or until all liquid is absorbed and rice is tender. Fold in parsley and pine nuts and fluff grains with a fork.

# SHIITAKE, RED PEPPER AND GINGER PILAF

*Baking pilafs in the oven yields a lovely, nonsticky texture. Serve this with bean or dairy dishes to make a complete protein.*

1 tbs. butter
1 tbs. olive oil
1 cup finely chopped red bell pepper
1/4 lb. shiitake mushrooms, stemmed and sliced
2 tsp. grated fresh ginger
1 1/2 cups long-grain white rice
2 cups *Vegetable Stock*, page 6 or purchased
3/4 cup water
1/4 tsp. salt

Heat oven to 350°. In a 2-quart, heavy-bottomed, ovenproof saucepan, heat butter and oil over medium heat and sauté bell pepper, mushrooms and ginger for 2 minutes. Stir in rice and sauté until rice grains are dry and slightly golden. Add stock and water, bring to a boil and season with salt. Cover pan, place in oven and bake for 15 minutes, or until all liquid is absorbed and rice is tender. Fluff grains with a fork and serve.

# BULGUR AND MUSHROOM PILAF

Servings: 5-6

*Here's a nice summer supper dish that goes well with **Baked Eggs in Tomatoes**, page 54.*

3 tbs. butter
½ cup finely chopped onion
½ cup finely chopped green bell pepper
1 cup chopped mushrooms
1 large clove garlic, minced
1½ cups bulgur wheat

2½ cups *Vegetable Stock*, page 6 or
   purchased
salt to taste
2 tbs. minced fresh mint
2 tbs. minced fresh flat-leaf parsley

Heat oven to 350°. In a 2-quart heavy-bottomed saucepan, melt 2 tbs. of the butter over medium heat and sauté onion and bell pepper for 4 minutes. Add remaining 1 tbs. butter and sauté mushrooms and garlic until mushrooms are slightly softened. Stir in bulgur and sauté until grains are dry. Add stock, bring to a boil and season lightly with salt. Cover pan, place in oven and bake for 15 minutes, or until all liquid is absorbed and grains are tender. Fold in mint and parsley and fluff grains with a fork.

# TABBOULI

*This dish has scads of variations. It is typically made with bulgur, parsley, mint, olive oil and lots of lemon juice. The very fresh taste makes this a great picnic or lunch dish with sandwiches or soup.*

¾ cup bulgur wheat
2 cups boiling water
⅔ cup minced green onions
8 cherry tomatoes, cut into quarters
1 cup finely chopped cucumbers, optional
1½ cups packed minced fresh flat-leaf parsley
⅓ cup minced fresh mint
¼ cup extra virgin olive oil
⅓-½ cup fresh lemon juice, or more to taste
salt to taste

In a bowl, cover bulgur with boiling water. Let bulgur stand, covered, for 30 minutes, or until grains are tender; drain and press free of liquid. Transfer bulgur to a another bowl and fluff grains with a fork. Stir in onions, tomatoes, cucumbers, if using, parsley, mint and olive oil. Add lemon juice and salt and mix well. Let stand at room temperature for 1 hour before serving. Refrigerate for longer storage.

# LEGUMES AND TOFU

# LEGUMES AND TOFU IN A VEGETARIAN DIET

The world of legumes took on a new dimension when vegetarian cooking became mainstream in our culture, and especially when tofu moved west. When we speak of legumes, we are generally referring to beans, peas and lentils. Peanuts, too, are technically considered a legume.

Legumes are a remarkable source of protein, lacking only the essential amino acid *methionine*, which can be furnished by complementary servings of milk, cheese or whole grains. One exception is the soybean, which is considered to be a perfect protein. Soybeans' by-product, tofu, is rich in estrogen. Legumes are also an excellent source of B vitamins, as well as iron, potassium and calcium. In addition, they are excellent sources of fiber, are low in sodium and are cholesterol-free.

All beans, peas, and lentils should be rinsed and picked over before cooking, especially those that come in bulk. Dried beans should be soaked before cooking. Two soaking methods follow. It is a good idea to avoid adding salt to the legumes until they have cooked awhile, so as not to inhibit tenderizing. Also, acidic foods, such as tomatoes or vinegar, should only be added when the beans are tender. The flavor of legumes often benefits from a splash of vinegar, lime or lemon juice; just remember to add it last.

# COOKING DRIED BEANS

Soaking dried beans before cooking lowers their gas-producing qualities, reduces the cooking time and keeps the bean skins from separating from the flesh. Two main soaking methods follow.

**QUICK SOAK**: For every pound of beans, use 2 quarts water. Bring beans and water to a rolling boil in a large pot and boil for 2 minutes; remove from heat, cover and let stand for 1 hour. Drain beans well. Cook beans in a large pot with fresh cold water, using about 6 cups water for every pound of beans.

**OVERNIGHT SOAK**: For every pound of beans, use 6 cups water. Soak beans in water in a large container overnight in the refrigerator. Drain beans well. Cook beans in a pot with fresh cold water, using about 6 cups water for every pound of beans.

## COOKING TIMES
split peas and lentils: less than 1 hour; not necessary to soak
navy and kidney beans: 1 to 1½ hours
white, black, Great Northern, pink, pinto and red beans,
    and black-eyed peas: about 1½ hours
garbanzo beans: about 2 hours
soy beans: 3 or more hours
lima beans: less than 1 hour for baby limas; about 1½ hours for large limas

# SPICY BLACK BEANS

*To turn these beans into a substantial and balanced-protein meal, serve with cheese **Quesadillas**, page 68, and cole slaw.*

2 cups dried black beans, soaked (see
    page 102) and drained
8 cups cold water
2 tbs. corn oil
1 tbs. minced garlic
2 fresh jalapeño chiles, seeded and
    minced
1 tsp. dried oregano leaves

½ tsp. dried basil leaves
½ cup tomato paste
½ cup chopped fresh cilantro
salt to taste
lime juice to taste
minced green onions for garnish
sour cream for garnish

Place drained, soaked beans and cold water in a large pot and bring to a boil. Reduce heat to low and simmer, covered, for about 1½ hours, until beans are tender.

In a small skillet, heat oil over medium heat and sauté garlic, jalapeños, oregano and basil until garlic is golden. Stir garlic mixture into cooked beans with tomato paste and cilantro. Stir in salt and lime juice. Serve beans in bowls garnished with green onions and dollops of sour cream.

# VEGETARIAN VEGETABLE CHILI

*This recipe can be varied endlessly, depending on which vegetables are in season or appeal to your family. Using canned beans makes the recipe a quickie to prepare.*

3 tbs. corn or canola oil
1 large onion, finely chopped
2 large cloves garlic, minced
1 large green or red bell pepper, finely
    chopped
1 stalk celery, finely chopped
1 medium carrot, finely chopped
2 tsp. chili powder
1 tsp. ground cumin
1 tsp. dried oregano leaves, crumbled
½ tsp. dried thyme leaves, crumbled
½ tsp. ground coriander
1 can (1 lb.) peeled tomatoes with
    juice, chopped

1 cup *Vegetable Stock*, page 6
    or purchased, or more if desired
2 cans (16 oz. each) pinto beans,
    rinsed and drained
1 cup fresh or frozen corn kernels
salt to taste
red wine vinegar to taste
1½ cups shredded sharp cheddar
    cheese
1½ cups finely shredded green
    cabbage
½ cup chopped fresh cilantro
2 jalapeño chiles, seeded and minced

In a large heavy-bottomed pot, heat oil over medium heat and sauté onion for 2 minutes. Add garlic and sauté until onion is almost tender. Add bell pepper, celery, carrot, chili powder, cumin, oregano, thyme and coriander and sauté for 3 minutes. Stir in tomatoes and stock and bring to a boil. Reduce heat to low and simmer, covered, for 10 minutes. Stir in beans and corn. Add salt, vinegar and additional stock, if you desire a soupier chili. Place cheese in a serving bowl. Toss cabbage with cilantro and place in a separate serving bowl. Place minced jalapeños in a small dish. Serve chili in warm bowls and let diners garnish individual servings with cheese, cabbage mixture and jalapeños at the table.

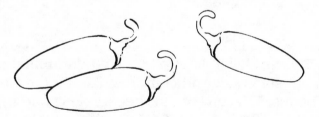

# REFRIED BEAN CASSEROLE

*Serve this with warm corn or flour tortillas for scooping, and a rice and vegetable salad.*

2 tbs. corn or canola oil
1 large onion, finely chopped
1 large green bell pepper, seeded, ribs removed and finely chopped
2 large cloves garlic, minced
1 tsp. ground cumin
1 can (2 lb.) vegetarian refried beans
2 cups shredded sharp cheddar cheese
½ cup medium-spicy tomato salsa
½ cup sour cream
minced fresh cilantro for garnish

Heat oven to 375°. In a skillet, heat oil over medium heat and sauté onion, bell pepper and garlic until softened. Add cumin and sauté for 1 minute. Transfer mixture to a bowl with beans, 1⅓ cups of the cheese, salsa and sour cream. Stir to mix well and transfer to a shallow casserole. Top with remaining ⅔ cup cheese and cover with aluminum foil. Bake for 16 to 18 minutes, or until hot and bubbly. Garnish with cilantro.

# WHITE BEANS WITH MARJORAM

*A nice combination of flavors, this dish goes well with* **Melted Cheese Sandwiches with Sautéed Vegetables**, *page 66.*

1 lb. dried Great Northern beans, soaked (see page 102) and drained
3 cups cold *Vegetable Stock*, page 6 or purchased
3 cups water
2 tbs. olive oil
1 large onion, quartered and thinly sliced
4 cloves garlic, minced

1½ tbs. fresh marjoram leaves, or about 2 tsp. dried
1 bay leaf
2 lb. fresh tomatoes, cored, peeled, seeded and chopped
⅓ cup fresh flat-leaf parsley leaves
salt to taste
lemon juice to taste
12 pitted Greek olives

In a large pot, bring drained soaked beans, stock and water to a boil. Reduce heat to low and simmer, covered, until beans are just tender, but not mushy. In a skillet, heat oil over medium heat and sauté onion for 4 minutes. Add garlic, marjoram and bay leaf and sauté for 2 minutes. Transfer onion mixture, tomatoes and parsley to pot with beans and simmer for 20 minutes, or until beans are tender. Stir in salt, lemon juice and olives. Serve in shallow bowls.

# POCKET BREADS WITH HUMMUS
# AND TOMATO-OLIVE RELISH

*These make a nice summer lunch with fresh fruit. Or, serve these with a soup for supper.*

1 can (15 oz.) garbanzo beans
1/4 cup fresh lemon juice, or more to taste
1 tbs. tahini (sesame seed paste)
2 cloves garlic, minced
dash cayenne pepper
4 whole wheat pita breads, warmed
*Tomato-Olive Relish*, follows
1/2 cup crumbled feta cheese

Drain beans, reserving 2 tbs. bean liquid. With a food processor, process beans, bean liquid, lemon juice, tahini, garlic and cayenne until well blended, scraping sides of machine as needed. Cut pita breads in half. Place hummus into pockets of pita bread halves, dividing evenly. Top hummus with *Tomato-Olive Relish* and crumbled feta cheese.

## TOMATO-OLIVE RELISH

1 large ripe tomato, peeled, cored, seeded and chopped
¾ cup finely chopped peeled and seeded cucumber
¼ cup chopped kalamata or other Greek olives
¼ cup minced green onions
2 tbs. minced fresh cilantro
salt to taste

In a bowl, toss together tomato, cucumber, olives, onions and cilantro. Stir in salt.

# LENTIL POCKET BURGERS
# WITH TOMATO-CUCUMBER RELISH

Servings: 6

*Consider accompanying these with soup or cole slaw.*

1 cup lentils
3 cups cold water, or more if needed
½ cup sunflower kernels
½ cup dry whole wheat breadcrumbs
2 large cloves garlic, minced
½ tsp. dried oregano leaves
½ tsp. dried basil

salt and freshly ground pepper to taste
red wine vinegar to taste
2 eggs, lightly beaten
canola oil
6 pita breads, warmed
*Tomato-Cucumber Relish*, follows

In a saucepan, bring lentils and water to a boil. Reduce heat to low and simmer, covered, for about 35 to 40 minutes, until lentils are tender. Add more water if necessary so lentils do not dry out. Drain lentils and transfer to a bowl. Stir in sunflower kernels, breadcrumbs, garlic, oregano and basil. Stir in salt, pepper and enough wine vinegar to make mixture slightly tangy. Stir in eggs until well mixed. When cool enough to handle, shape lentil mixture into 6 soft patties.

110   LEGUMES AND TOFU

In a skillet, heat a small amount of oil over medium-high heat and cook patties until browned on both sides and heated through. Cut a small portion from the top of each pita bread so that a lentil patty can be inserted inside. Place patties inside warmed pita breads and top with *Tomato-Cucumber Relish*.

## TOMATO-CUCUMBER RELISH

Makes about 3 cups

2 ripe medium tomatoes, peeled, cored, seeded and finely
    chopped
½ medium cucumber, peeled, seeded and finely chopped
2 tbs. minced onion
1 large clove garlic, minced
2 tbs. minced fresh cilantro
1½ cups nonfat plain yogurt
salt to taste

In a bowl, mix tomatoes, cucumber, onion, garlic and cilantro. Stir in yogurt and salt. Chill until ready to serve.

# LENTIL AND BULGUR SALAD

*As a lunch or light supper, this dish is nice with melted cheese sandwiches.*

1 cup lentils
3 cups cold water, or more if needed
1 cup bulgur wheat
2 cups boiling water
1 cup chopped fresh flat-leaf parsley
1 cup finely chopped sweet red onion
1½ cups finely chopped baby spinach leaves
*Creamy Lemon Dressing*, page 53, to taste

In a saucepan, bring lentils and 3 cups water to a boil. Reduce heat to low and simmer, covered, for 35 to 40 minutes, until lentils are tender. Add more water if necessary so lentils do not dry out. Drain lentils and transfer to a bowl.

While lentils are cooking, place bulgur in a bowl, cover with 2 cups boiling water and let stand for 30 minutes, or until tender. Drain bulgur, press free of liquid and fluff grains with a fork. Transfer bulgur to bowl with lentils and mix well. Cover bowl and chill for 1 hour. To bowl, add parsley and onion and mix well. Fold in spinach leaves and toss with *Creamy Lemon Dressing*.

# LIMA BEAN SALAD

*Complete a summer dinner by serving this salad with grilled cheese sandwiches on whole wheat bread. Take care not to overcook the lima beans, or they will turn mushy and lose their skins.*

2 cups dried baby lima beans, soaked (see page 102) and drained
4 cups cold water
1 small sweet red onion, quartered and thinly sliced
2/3 cup diced celery
1 bunch watercress, tough stems removed, chopped
½ cup large pitted ripe olives, halved
1 tbs. fresh thyme leaves, or 1 tsp. dried
*Garlic-Mustard Vinaigrette*, page 117, to taste
salt and freshly ground pepper to taste
butter lettuce leaves

In a large saucepan, bring drained soaked beans and water to a boil. Reduce heat to low and simmer, covered, for about 50 to 60 minutes, until tender; take care not to overcook. Drain beans well and transfer to a bowl. While warm, toss beans with onion, celery, watercress, olives and thyme. Add *Garlic-Mustard Vinaigrette*, salt and pepper and toss well. Serve at room temperature on lettuce leaves.

# PEPPER AND BEAN SALAD
# WITH CREAMY LIME DRESSING

Servings: 4-5

*For a company lunch, serve this attractive, quick-to-prepare salad with sliced cheese and corn muffins or quesadillas. If possible, use green, red and yellow bell peppers.*

2 tbs. olive oil
3 large bell peppers, seeded, ribs removed and coarsely chopped
2 cloves garlic, minced
1 can (15 oz.) pinto beans
1 can (16 oz.) black beans
1 cup coarsely chopped green onions
*Creamy Lime Dressing*, follows
salt and freshly ground pepper to taste
fresh cilantro leaves for garnish

In a nonstick skillet, heat olive oil over medium heat and sauté peppers and garlic until peppers are crisp-tender. Transfer sautéed peppers to a bowl. Combine pinto and black beans in a colander and rinse well with cold water; drain well and add to bowl with peppers and onions.

Add dressing to bowl with bean-pepper mixture, season with salt and pepper and toss well. Cover salad and refrigerate until well chilled. Serve garnished with cilantro.

## CREAMY LIME DRESSING

Makes about 1 cup

1/3 cup canola oil
3 tbs. fresh lime juice
2 tbs. mayonnaise
3 tbs. minced fresh cilantro
1/2 tsp. ground cumin
salt and freshly ground pepper to taste

In a bowl, whisk together canola oil, lime juice, mayonnaise, cilantro and cumin until blended. Season with salt and pepper.

# WHITE BEAN SALAD WITH GARLIC-MUSTARD VINAIGRETTE

*Serve this as a summer supper with grilled cheese sandwiches on whole wheat bread.*

3/4 cups dried Great Northern beans, soaked (see page 102) and drained
3 cups cold water
*Garlic-Mustard Vinaigrette*, follows
1 tbs. olive oil
1 medium-sized sweet red onion, quartered and thinly sliced
1 large red bell pepper, quartered, seeded, ribs removed and thinly sliced
1/2 cup fresh flat-leaf parsley leaves
1 tsp. dried oregano leaves
2/3 cup pimiento-stuffed olives
salt and freshly ground pepper to taste
romaine lettuce leaves

In a large saucepan, bring drained soaked beans and water to a boil. Reduce heat to low and simmer, covered, for about 1½ hours, until tender. Drain beans well and transfer to a bowl. While warm, toss beans with a small amount of *Garlic Mustard Vinaigrette*. In a small skillet, heat oil over medium heat and sauté onion, bell pepper, parsley and oregano until vegetables are crisp-tender. Add vegetable mixture to bean mixture with olives and mix well. Add additional dressing to taste and season with salt and pepper. Serve at room temperature on lettuce leaves.

## GARLIC-MUSTARD VINAIGRETTE

Makes about 1⅔ cups

1 egg yolk*
½ cup red wine vinegar
2 tbs. Dijon mustard
4 cloves garlic, minced
1 cup olive oil
salt and freshly ground pepper to taste

In a bowl, whisk egg yolk with vinegar, mustard and garlic. Add oil and continue to whisk until well blended. Season with salt and pepper.

*Some health authorities discourage using raw eggs in recipes due to a minimal risk of bacterial contamination.

# ITALIAN NAVY BEAN SALAD

*This makes a savory summer supper served with a chilled soup, hot whole grain rolls and sliced cheese.*

1⅔ cups dried navy beans, soaked (see page 102) and drained
5 cups cold water
1 cup fresh flat-leaf parsley leaves
½ cup olive oil
2 tbs. balsamic vinegar
2 tbs. snipped chives

2 large cloves garlic, pressed
1 tsp. dried oregano leaves
1 tsp. dried basil leaves
½ tsp. salt
½ tsp. sugar
salt and freshly ground pepper to taste
fresh baby spinach leaves

In a large saucepan, bring drained, soaked beans and water to a boil. Reduce heat to low and simmer, covered, for 1 to 1½ hours, until beans are tender. Drain beans well, transfer to a bowl and toss with parsley leaves. In a jar with a tight-fitting lid, combine oil, vinegar, chives, garlic, oregano, basil, ½ tsp. salt and sugar; shake well. While warm, toss beans with dressing and season with salt and pepper. Serve at room temperature on a bed of fresh spinach leaves.

# BOMBAY CHICKPEAS AND POTATOES

*Chickpeas is another term for garbanzo beans. Serve this dish over rice accompanied by chutney, a cucumber-yogurt salad and toasted whole wheat pita bread.*

3 medium russet potatoes
2 tsp. butter
2 large onions, chopped
3 cloves garlic, minced
2 tsp. whole cumin seeds
1 tsp. ground coriander
½ tsp. turmeric
½ tsp. powdered ginger

⅛ tsp. cinnamon
1 can (15 oz.) garbanzo beans, rinsed
   and drained
1 can (15 oz.) crushed tomatoes
1½ cups *Vegetable Stock*, page 6 or
   purchased, or use part water
½ tsp. salt, or to taste

Peel potatoes, quarter lengthwise and cut into ½-inch slices. In a large nonstick skillet, melt butter over medium-low heat and sauté onions and garlic for 6 minutes. Add cumin seeds, coriander, turmeric, ginger and cinnamon and sauté for 2 minutes, stirring constantly. Add potatoes to skillet and cook for 5 minutes, turning frequently. Stir in garbanzo beans, tomatoes and stock and simmer until potatoes are tender. Season with salt. Serve immediately.

# BLACK BEAN BURRITOS
# WITH SALSA VERDE

*This makes a delicious winter or summer supper with a rice or bulgur wheat salad. Look for tomatillos in the Mexican food section of the supermarket or in a Latin American market.*

6 large flour tortillas
1 tbs. corn or canola oil
1 cup minced onion
1 cup finely chopped green bell pepper
2 cloves garlic, minced
1 tsp. ground cumin
2 cups rinsed, well-drained canned black beans
1½ cups cooked white rice
1½ cups crumbled Mexican white cheese (queso fresco) or feta cheese
*Salsa Verde*, follows

Heat oven to 350°. Wrap tortillas with aluminum foil and bake for 15 minutes, until warmed through; keep warm. In a 12-inch nonstick skillet, heat oil over medium heat and sauté onion, green pepper, garlic and cumin until vegetables are crisp-tender. Stir in beans and rice and cook until mixture is heated through.

Place warmed tortillas on a work surface. Spread bean and rice mixture down the middle of each tortilla, dividing evenly. Sprinkle each burrito with a small amount of cheese and top with a small amount of *Salsa Verde*. Fold sides of tortillas in towards the center. Fold the bottoms of tortillas up over the filling. Gently, but tightly, roll tortillas up to the top edge. Serve immediately.

## SALSA VERDE
Makes about 1½ cups

1 can (10 or 13 oz.) tomatillos
¼ corn or canola oil
1 small onion, finely chopped
2 cloves garlic, minced
2 jalapeño chiles, seeded and chopped
3 tbs. minced fresh cilantro
salt to taste

Drain tomatillos well and process with a blender or food processor until well blended. In a skillet, heat oil over medium heat and sauté onion for 4 minutes. Add garlic and sauté for 2 minutes. Stir in blended tomatillos and simmer mixture for 5 minutes. Remove skillet from heat and stir in jalapeños and cilantro. Season with salt.

# SPICY PINTO BEAN TACOS

*Tacos are always a popular supper dish; these go nicely with a rice salad.*

1 tbs. corn or canola oil
1 cup finely chopped onion
1 cup finely chopped green bell pepper
1 large clove garlic, minced
2½ cups drained, canned pinto beans,
   bean liquid reserved
1 tsp. dried oregano leaves

1 tsp. ground cumin
2 cups crumbled fresh Mexican white
   cheese (queso fresco) or feta cheese
*Fresh Tomato Salsa*, page 85
3 cups finely shredded lettuce
12 corn tortillas

In a 12-inch nonstick skillet, heat oil over medium heat and sauté onion, bell pepper and garlic until vegetables are crisp-tender. Stir in beans, oregano, cumin and enough of the bean liquid to moisten ingredients. Cook mixture until heated through, remove from heat and keep warm.

When ready to eat, place bowls of cheese, salsa and lettuce on the table. Cook tortillas directly on a hot electric burner, gas burner or griddle, flipping back and forth until warm and flexible. Fill each tortilla with a generous amount of bean filling. Let diners add cheese, salsa and lettuce to their tacos at the table.

# TOFU AND PEANUT RICE

*Serve this substantial entrée with whole wheat bread, a yogurt-cucumber salad and sliced tomatoes or tomato chutney.*

2 tbs. canola oil
1 cup finely chopped green onions
1 cup finely chopped red bell pepper
1 tbs. minced garlic
3 cups shredded fresh spinach leaves
1 tsp. grated fresh ginger
4 cups cooked brown or white rice
12 oz. firm tofu, diced
1 cup dry-roasted peanuts
3-4 tbs. soy sauce

In a 12-inch nonstick skillet, heat oil over medium heat and sauté onions, bell pepper and garlic for 4 minutes. Stir in spinach and sauté until just wilted. Add ginger and rice and mix well. Stir in tofu and peanuts. Season with soy sauce to taste and cook until mixture is heated through. Serve immediately.

# MUSHROOM, RICE AND TOFU LOAF

*This makes a lovely company or family meal with cheesy scalloped potatoes, steamed vegetables and a tossed green salad. Serve whole grain rolls on the side. Look for powdered vegetable broth in jars or bulk bins in a natural food store.*

8 dried shiitake mushrooms
3 cups warm water, plus more if needed
3 tbs. soy sauce
3 tbs. powdered vegetable broth
1½ cups long-grain and wild rice mix
2 tbs. canola oil
1 cup finely chopped onion
¼ lb. white mushrooms, chopped
4 medium cloves garlic, minced

10 oz. firm tofu
1 cup fine soft breadcrumbs
1 cup freshly grated Asiago or Parmesan cheese
2 eggs, beaten
½ cup sunflower kernels, toasted
1 tbs. dried thyme leaves
½ tsp. coarsely ground pepper
salt to taste

In a bowl, soak shiitake mushrooms in warm water and soy sauce for 30 minutes; drain mushrooms well, reserving liquid, and chop finely. Measure liquid, adding additional water if necessary to equal 3 cups. In a large saucepan, bring mushroom liquid, powdered vegetable broth and rice to a boil. Reduce heat to very low and simmer, covered, for 30 minutes, or until rice is tender and liquid is absorbed.

Heat oven to 350°. In a skillet, heat oil over medium-high heat and sauté onion, white mushrooms and garlic until softened. Transfer mixture to a bowl with cooked rice, shiitake mushrooms, tofu, breadcrumbs, cheese, eggs, sunflower kernels, thyme and pepper. Mix well and season with salt. Transfer mixture to a buttered 10-inch pie pan and bake for 35 to 50 minutes, or until firm and lightly browned. Cut into wedges to serve.

# VEGETABLE SCRAMBLED TOFU

*For a savory, satisfying meal, serve this with a green salad and whole grain bread. This recipe is easy to double or triple when serving a crowd. You can use any favored vegetables in this, especially those that are seasonal. Choose tofu that is labeled "firm" or "extra-firm," as it holds its shape better than softer varieties. A secret: add the tofu to the dish early so that it picks up the other flavors.*

2 tbs. olive oil
1/4 cup thinly sliced green onions
1 tbs. minced garlic
3/4 cup diced green bell pepper (about 1 small pepper)
10 oz. red potatoes (about 2 large), diced
1/2 tsp. dried oregano leaves, crumbled
1/2 tsp. dried thyme leaves, crumbled
1/2 tsp. dried basil leaves, crumbled
2 tbs. finely chopped fresh cilantro
8 oz. firm tofu, diced
2 cups diced zucchini
2 tbs. seasoned rice vinegar
salt to taste
red pepper flakes to taste

In a large nonstick skillet, heat oil over medium heat and sauté onions and garlic for 2 minutes. Add bell pepper, potatoes, oregano, thyme, basil, cilantro and tofu and sauté until potatoes are almost tender. Add zucchini and sauté until zucchini is crisp-tender and potatoes are tender, but not mushy. Stir in rice vinegar, salt and red pepper flakes. Serve immediately.

# TOFU BURGERS

Makes 5

*Serve these with soup or steamed vegetables and a salad. Or, serve them in pita bread with **Tomato-Cucumber Relish**, page 111, or in buns with "the works." To achieve a texture that is like ground meat, freeze purchased tofu for 3 days, thaw it in the refrigerator and press it free of liquid before crumbling.*

2 tbs. olive oil, plus more for frying
½ cup finely chopped onion
½ cup finely chopped green bell pepper
½ cup finely chopped celery
2 large cloves garlic, minced
½ cup minced fresh flat-leaf parsley
½ tsp. dried oregano leaves, crumbled
½ tsp. dried thyme leaves, crumbled
½ tsp. dried basil leaves, crumbled
1 lb. firm tofu, frozen, thawed, pressed free of liquid and crumbled
¼ cup freshly grated Parmesan cheese
salt and freshly ground pepper to taste
1 egg, lightly beaten
unbleached all-purpose flour
5 pita breads or sandwich buns

In a skillet, heat 2 tbs. oil over medium heat and sauté onion, bell pepper, celery and garlic for 2 minutes. Add parsley, oregano, thyme and basil and sauté until vegetables are softened. Transfer mixture to a bowl with tofu and cheese and mix well. Season with salt and pepper. Add egg and enough flour so patties hold their shape. Form mixture into 5 patties.

In a skillet, heat a small amount of olive oil over medium-high heat. Fry patties until lightly browned on both sides and heated through. Serve immediately in pita breads or sandwich buns.

# TOFU TACOS

*Serve these with a green salad and fresh fruit. Freezing and thawing fresh tofu gives it a texture like ground meat when crumbled. Purchase tofu at the supermarket, freeze it for 3 days in its original package and thaw it in the refrigerator.*

2 tbs. canola or corn oil
1 cup finely chopped onion
1 cup chopped green bell pepper
2 large cloves garlic, minced
1 lb. firm tofu, frozen, thawed,
   pressed free of liquid and crumbled
1½ tsp. dried oregano leaves

salt to taste
1½ cups shredded sharp cheddar
   cheese
*Fresh Tomato Salsa*, page 85
2 cups finely shredded lettuce
12 corn tortillas

In a skillet, heat oil over medium heat and sauté onion and bell pepper for 2 minutes. Add garlic and cook until vegetables are soft and garlic is golden. Add tofu and oregano and sauté until heated through. Season with salt, remove from heat and keep warm.

When ready to eat, place bowls of cheese, salsa and lettuce on the table. Cook tortillas directly on a hot electric burner, gas burner or griddle, flipping back and forth until warm and flexible. Fill each tortilla with a generous amount of filling. Let diners add cheese, salsa and lettuce to their tacos at the table.

# TOFU AND BEAN BURRITOS

*Pair these with fresh fruit for lunch. Add a soup, chilled or hot, to the menu for supper. Freeze fresh tofu for 3 days in its package and thaw it in the refrigerator.*

12 large flour tortillas
2 tbs. canola or corn oil
1 cup chopped onion
1 cup chopped red bell pepper
2 large cloves garlic, minced
12 oz. firm tofu, frozen, thawed, pressed free of liquid and crumbled
1 tsp. dried marjoram leaves

½ tsp. ground cumin
1 cup drained cooked or canned kidney beans
*Salsa Verde*, page 121, to taste
salt to taste
1½ cups crumbled fresh Mexican white cheese (queso fresco) or feta cheese

Heat oven to 350°. Wrap tortillas with aluminum foil and bake for 15 minutes, until warmed through; keep warm. In a skillet, heat oil over medium heat and sauté onion and bell pepper for 2 minutes. Add garlic and sauté until vegetables are soft and garlic is golden. Add tofu, marjoram and cumin and sauté for a few minutes. Stir in beans and heat through. Stir in salsa and salt. Lay tortillas on a work surface and spread filling down the middle of each tortilla, dividing evenly. Sprinkle with cheese. Fold sides of tortillas in towards the center. Fold the bottom of tortillas up over the filling. Gently, but tightly, roll tortilla up to the top edge. Serve immediately.

# PASTA

# PASTA IN A VEGETARIAN DIET

In the vegetarian arena, pasta is a great food base for creative cooking. Not only can we get a lot of good-quality imported wheat pastas these days, but the U.S. is producing delicious pastas made from whole wheat, vegetables, wheat, soy flour, corn and rice.

All packaged pastas list preparation times, but it is important not to overcook pasta. The Italians describe perfectly cooked pasta as *al dente,* which means "to the tooth." Pasta cooked al dente should have just a slight resistance when bitten.

Other secrets to a good pasta dish are: always grate your dry cheeses — Parmesan, Romano or Asiago — as you need them; and always use a good-quality olive oil.

If a pasta dish ever seems dry, just add a bit of vegetable broth to moisten it. Prepare for this by making a big pot of *Vegetable Stock*, page 6, pouring the cooled stock into ice cube trays and freezing until solid. Transfer the vegetable stock cubes to a locking plastic freezer bag when frozen and thaw a cube or two as needed.

# SPINACH LASAGNA

*Serve this vegetarian version of an Italian-American classic with a tossed salad and crisp sliced bread.*

9 lasagna noodles
3 large bunches spinach
2 tbs. olive oil
1 cup chopped onion
1 tbs. minced garlic
2 cans (8 oz. each) tomato sauce
1 can (6 oz.) tomato paste
1 cup water
1 tsp. dried oregano leaves, crumbled
½ tsp. dried thyme leaves, crumbled
½ tsp. dried basil leaves, crumbled
¼ tsp. cinnamon
salt and freshly ground pepper to taste
1 egg
1 lb. ricotta cheese
2 cups shredded mozzarella cheese
1 cup freshly grated Parmesan cheese

In a large pot of boiling salted water, cook lasagna noodles according to package directions. Drain and set aside.

Trim spinach, wash well and spin dry. Steam spinach briefly, just until wilted; set aside. In a medium skillet, heat oil over medium heat and sauté onion and garlic until onion is translucent and garlic is golden. Stir in tomato sauce, tomato paste, water, oregano, thyme, basil and cinnamon. Season with salt and pepper and simmer, uncovered, over very low heat for 10 minutes.

Heat oven to 375°. In a bowl, beat egg with ricotta cheese until well blended. Lay 3 of the cooked lasagna noodles in a buttered 9-x-13-inch baking dish. Spread noodles with ⅓ of the tomato sauce; top with ½ of the ricotta mixture. Arrange ½ of the spinach over ricotta mixture and sprinkle with ½ of the mozzarella cheese. Repeat layering process. Top with remaining pasta, remaining sauce and Parmesan cheese. Cover dish with aluminum foil and bake for 20 minutes. Remove cover and bake for 15 to 20 minutes, or until lasagna is heated through and cheese is melted.

# VEGETABLE LASAGNA

*You can't have too many lasagna recipes! A green salad and hot bread will make this one into a complete meal.*

5 tbs. olive oil
1 large onion, chopped
2 tbs. minced garlic
1 eggplant, about 1 lb., peeled and
   diced
2 tsp. dried oregano leaves, crumbled
½ tsp. dried thyme leaves, crumbled
½ tsp. dried basil, crumbled
2 cups sliced mushrooms
1 can (1 lb.) Italian plum tomatoes
1 can (8 oz.) tomato sauce
½ cup dry red wine, optional

½ cup chopped fresh flat-leaf parsley
   leaves
salt and freshly ground pepper to taste
12 lasagna noodles
1 egg
1 lb. ricotta cheese
8 oz. mozzarella cheese, thinly sliced
2 cups grated Parmesan cheese

In a large skillet, heat oil over medium heat and sauté onion for 3 minutes. Add garlic and eggplant and sauté until eggplant begins to soften. Stir in oregano, thyme, basil and mushrooms and sauté until eggplant is fork-tender. Add tomatoes, breaking up with a fork or your hands. Stir in tomato sauce, wine, if using, and parsley and bring to a boil. Reduce heat to low and simmer, covered, for 15 minutes, seasoning with salt and pepper.

In a large pot of boiling salted water, cook lasagna noodles according to package directions. Drain noodles and set aside.

Heat oven to 350°. In a bowl, beat egg with ricotta cheese until well blended. Spread ¼ of the vegetable sauce in a 9-x-13-inch baking dish and arrange 3 of the cooked lasagna noodles on top. With a butter knife, carefully spread ⅓ of the ricotta mixture over noodles. Sprinkle with ⅓ of the mozzarella cheese and ¼ of the Parmesan cheese. Repeat layering process 2 times. Top with remaining ¼ of the vegetable sauce and remaining ¼ of the Parmesan cheese. Cover dish with aluminum foil and bake for 20 minutes. Remove cover and bake for 5 to 10 minutes, or until lasagna is heated through and cheese is melted.

# CHEESE-FILLED MANICOTTI

*Children love these fat little pasta tubes; and they are not exclusively a kid's meal. Serve them with a spinach salad and whole grain rolls.*

4 cups ricotta cheese
8 oz. mozzarella cheese, shredded
2 eggs
½ cup freshly grated Parmesan cheese
¼ cup minced fresh flat-leaf parsley,
   plus more for garnish
salt and freshly ground pepper to taste
1 pkg. (8 oz.) manicotti
¼ cup butter
2 tbs. unbleached all-purpose flour
2 cups milk

Bring a large pot of salted water to a boil. Heat oven to 375°. In a bowl, combine ricotta, mozzarella, eggs, ¼ cup of the Parmesan and parsley. Beat to mix well and season with salt and pepper; set aside.

Cook manicotti in boiling water according to package directions; drain, rinse with warm water and drain again (cold water makes them break).

In a saucepan, melt butter over medium heat. Add flour and sauté for 1 minute. Slowly add milk and cook until mixture is heated through and thickened. Add remaining ¼ cup Parmesan cheese and season with salt; remove from heat. Spoon a thin layer of cheese sauce in a 9-x-13-inch baking dish. With a small spoon, carefully stuff cooled manicotti shells with cheese mixture and lay in dish. Cover stuffed shells with remaining sauce. Cover dish lightly with aluminum foil and bake for about 20 minutes, until hot and bubbly. Garnish with minced parsley. Serve immediately.

# TOFU- AND SPINACH-STUFFED MANICOTTI

*Serve this dish with steamed yellow vegetables and hot rolls.*

8 manicotti noodles
¼ cup olive oil
¼ cup minced onion
2 tbs. minced garlic
½ tsp. dried oregano leaves
1½ tsp. dried basil leaves
2 tbs. minced fresh flat-leaf parsley
1 lb. tofu
1 pkg. (10 oz.) frozen chopped
    spinach, thawed
1 egg
salt and freshly ground pepper to taste
3 large tomatoes, cored, peeled,
    seeded and chopped
red pepper flakes to taste
¼ cup freshly grated Parmesan cheese

In a large pot of boiling salted water, cook manicotti according to package directions; drain, rinse in warm water and drain again (cold water makes them break).

In a skillet, heat 2 tbs. of the oil over medium heat and sauté onion, 1 tbs. of the garlic, oregano, ½ tsp. of the basil and parsley for 2 minutes. Transfer onion mixture to a bowl with tofu, spinach and egg. Beat to mix well and season with salt and pepper; set aside. In a large nonstick skillet, heat remaining 2 tbs. oil over medium heat and sauté remaining 1 tbs. garlic until golden; stir in tomatoes and remaining 1 tsp. basil and simmer, covered, for 10 minutes. Season with salt and pepper flakes.

Heat oven to 375°. With a small spoon, carefully stuff manicotti shells with tofu stuffing. Arrange stuffed shells in a 9-x-13-inch baking dish, pour tomato sauce over the top and sprinkle with cheese. Cover dish with foil and bake, covered, for 20 minutes, until hot throughout. Serve immediately.

# RIGATONI WITH EGGPLANT

*Accompany this substantial entrée with good crusty bread and a tossed green salad.*

5 tbs. olive oil
1 medium onion, coarsely chopped
1 eggplant, about 1 lb., peeled and
  diced
2 tbs. minced garlic
1 can (1 lb.) plum tomatoes
1 can (6 oz.) tomato paste
2½ cups water
2 tsp. brown sugar
½ cup pitted kalamata olives

1 tsp. dried oregano leaves
½ tsp. dried basil leaves
½ tsp. cinnamon
¼ tsp. fennel seeds
½ cup dry white wine
⅓ lb. mushrooms, sliced
salt and red pepper flakes to taste
12 oz. rigatoni
freshly grated Parmesan cheese

Bring a large pot of salted water to a boil. In a heavy nonstick skillet, heat 2 tbs. of the olive oil over medium heat and sauté onion for 4 minutes. With a slotted spoon, transfer onion to a plate. Add remaining 3 tbs. oil to skillet and sauté eggplant with garlic for 5 minutes. Return onion to skillet with tomatoes, tomato paste, water, sugar, olives, oregano, basil, cinnamon and fennel seeds and bring to a boil. Reduce heat to low and simmer, covered, for 40 minutes. Stir in wine and mushrooms and simmer for 10 minutes. Season with salt and pepper flakes.

Cook rigatoni in boiling water according to package directions; drain. Transfer pasta to a warm serving platter or individual plates and top with sauce. Pass Parmesan cheese at the table.

# RIGATONI WITH BROCCOLI
# AND BLUE CHEESE

*This satisfying dish is definitely not for the faint-hearted, nor anyone on a low-cholesterol diet. Serve it with a green salad and hot bread.*

1 lb. rigatoni
2 tbs. butter
2 tbs. canola oil
2 cups chopped broccoli
2/3 cup crumbled Danish blue cheese
1½ cups half-and-half
½ lb. cherry tomatoes

In a large pot of boiling salted water, cook rigatoni according to package directions; drain and set aside. In a large skillet, heat butter and oil over medium-high heat and sauté broccoli until crisp-tender. In a saucepan over very low heat, stir cheese and half-and-half until cheese is melted. Add cooked pasta to skillet with broccoli and heat through. Transfer to a warm serving platter or individual plates and pour cheese sauce over rigatoni. Top with cherry tomatoes.

# LINGUINE WITH PESTO

*This pesto recipe makes 1 cup, more than you will need for a light pasta dish. It keeps well, though, and can be frozen. Bring frozen pesto to room temperature before using. Try this dish with a hearty soup, chilled or hot, and with a substantial bread.*

⅓ cup pine nuts
2½ cups fresh basil leaves
4 large cloves garlic
½-¾ cup olive oil

¼ cup freshly grated Parmesan cheese,
   plus more for passing
salt and freshly ground pepper to taste
8-10 oz. linguine

In a small skillet over medium heat, sauté pine nuts for 1 to 2 minutes, or until slightly browned; remove from heat. With a blender, process pine nuts, basil, garlic, ½ cup of the olive oil and ¼ cup Parmesan cheese until combined, but still with some texture. Add enough of the remaining olive oil to achieve the consistency of heavy cream. Season with salt and pepper. In a large pot of boiling salted water, cook linguine according to package directions; drain. Toss pasta with pesto to taste and pass extra Parmesan cheese at the table. Transfer unused pesto to a covered container and refrigerate or freeze until ready to use.

# RICE PASTA WITH EGGPLANT PESTO

*Eggplant is an interesting addition to traditional basil pesto. Look for rice pasta in natural food stores and some supermarkets. Serve this dish with a tossed green salad and country-style bread. Make the pesto first.*

7 oz. rice pasta or fusilli
2 tbs. olive oil
1 small sweet onion, finely chopped
3 large cloves garlic, minced
*Eggplant Pesto*, follows
*Vegetable Stock*, page 6 or purchased
grated Asiago cheese

Bring a large pot of boiling salted water to a boil. Cook pasta in boiling water according to package directions; drain and set aside. In a skillet, heat oil over medium-high heat and sauté onion and garlic until lightly browned and soft. Stir in *Eggplant Pesto*, and enough stock to make a thick sauce that will cling to pasta. Add pasta to skillet and toss well. Serve hot topped with cheese.

## EGGPLANT PESTO

¾ lb. eggplant, peeled and diced (about 3 cups)
salt
¼ cup olive oil
1 cup chopped onion
2 large cloves garlic, chopped
1 cup fresh basil leaves, loosely packed
¾ cup walnuts
3 oz. grated Asiago cheese
1 tbs. balsamic vinegar

Place eggplant in a colander and sprinkle generously with salt; let stand over the sink for 20 minutes. In a nonstick skillet, heat 2 tbs. of the olive oil over medium heat and sauté onion and garlic for 2 minutes. Add remaining 2 tbs. oil and drained eggplant and sauté until eggplant is lightly browned and soft. Transfer ingredients to a food processor workbowl with basil, walnuts, cheese and vinegar. Process mixture until well blended, but still with some texture. Transfer pesto to a small dish and set aside.

# CREMINI MUSHROOMS
# WITH BEANS AND PENNE

*Cremini (brown) mushrooms have a richer flavor than standard white mushrooms. Combined with garbanzo beans, they add an exotic touch to pasta. Serve this dish with a mixed green salad and toasted pita bread.*

2 tbs. butter
1 tbs. olive oil
½ cup chopped green onions, white part only
2 large cloves garlic, minced
1 tsp. ground cumin
½ tsp. ground coriander
½ lb. cremini (brown) mushrooms, sliced
1 cup fresh flat-leaf parsley leaves
½ cup lemon juice
½ cup *Vegetable Stock*, page 6 or purchased
1 can (15 oz.) garbanzo beans, rinsed and drained
1 tsp. sugar
salt and freshly ground pepper to taste
red pepper flakes to taste
8 oz. penne

Bring a large pot of salted water to a boil. In a large skillet, heat butter and oil over medium heat and sauté onions, garlic, cumin and coriander for 2 minutes. Add mushrooms and sauté for 2 minutes. Add parsley, lemon juice and stock and simmer, covered, for 5 minutes. Stir in garbanzo beans and sugar and cook until heated through. Season with salt, pepper and red pepper flakes; remove from heat.

Cook penne in boiling water according to package directions; drain. Add penne to skillet with vegetables and cook until heated through.

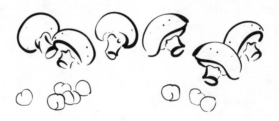

# PENNE WITH FRESH
# VEGETABLES AND HERBS

*This nice summer pasta goes well with a tomato salad and bakery-style bread.*

¼ cup olive oil
2 medium very sweet onions, thinly sliced
2 tbs. minced garlic
1 medium-sized red bell pepper, seeded, ribs
    removed and cut into penne-sized strips
1 medium-sized yellow bell pepper, seeded, ribs
    removed and cut into penne-sized strips
½ lb. cremini (brown) mushrooms, sliced
3 tbs. fresh oregano leaves
⅓ cup fresh flat-leaf parsley leaves
1 tbs. balsamic vinegar
salt and freshly ground pepper to taste
1 lb. penne
*Vegetable Stock*, page 6 or purchased, to taste
1 cup freshly grated Asiago cheese

Bring a large pot of salted water to a boil. In a large skillet, heat oil over medium heat and sauté onions and garlic for 4 minutes. Add bell peppers and mushrooms and sauté until peppers are crisp-tender. Add oregano and parsley and sauté for 1 minute. Stir in vinegar and season lightly with salt and pepper.

Cook penne in boiling water according to package directions; drain. Transfer penne to skillet with vegetables, adding enough stock to moisten to your preference. Toss well and serve topped with Asiago cheese.

# SUMMER MACARONI AND CHEESE

*This makes a perfect one-dish meal for kids, and it gives an old favorite a nourishing twist. This dish can be made in advance and refrigerated, but it should be brought to room temperature before reheating. If cold, it will take a little longer to heat through.*

¼ cup butter
2 tbs. unbleached all-purpose flour
2 cups milk
3 cups shredded sharp cheddar cheese
dash cayenne pepper
1 lb. elbow macaroni
2 tbs. olive oil
1 large bunch Swiss chard, trimmed, chopped, well
    washed and spun dry (about 6 cups)
1½ cups chopped red bell peppers
2 cups chopped summer squash, such as zucchini or yellow crookneck
salt and red pepper flakes to taste
2 tbs. butter
1 large clove garlic, minced
3 cups soft breadcrumbs
3 tbs. grated Parmesan cheese

Bring a large pot of salted water to a boil. In a saucepan, melt ¼ cup butter over low heat, stir in flour and cook, stirring, for 1 minute. Slowly add milk to pan, stirring constantly until mixture is slightly thickened. Add cheese and stir until melted; remove from heat and stir in cayenne.

Cook macaroni in boiling water according to package directions; drain. Transfer macaroni to a buttered 9-x-13-inch baking dish and pour cheese sauce over the top; set aside.

Heat oven to 375°. In a large nonstick skillet, heat olive oil over medium-high heat and sauté chard, bell peppers and squash for about 8 to 10 minutes, until chard is tender. Season vegetables with salt and red pepper flakes. Spread vegetables evenly over macaroni and cheese sauce. In skillet, melt 2 tbs. butter and sauté garlic for 1 minute. Add breadcrumbs and sauté until breadcrumbs are coated and slightly cooked. Sprinkle breadcrumbs over vegetables and sprinkle Parmesan cheese over the top. Bake for 25 minutes, or until dish is bubbling and breadcrumbs are crisp.

# FAMILY MACARONI AND CHEESE

*This is a dish that the kids will like. For added nutrition, choose soy-wheat or sesame elbow macaroni. Look for it in natural food stores. Serve this dish with cole slaw and whole grain rolls.*

2 cups soy-wheat or sesame macaroni
3 tbs. butter or margarine
1 cup finely chopped green onions, white part only
1 cup finely chopped green bell pepper
2 tbs. unbleached all-purpose flour
1 cup low-fat milk
2 cups shredded sharp cheddar cheese
salt and cayenne pepper to taste
1 large clove garlic, minced
1½ cups fresh breadcrumbs
1 tbs. freshly grated Parmesan cheese

Heat oven to 350°. In a large pot of boiling salted water, cook macaroni according to package directions; drain. Transfer pasta to a buttered 1½-quart casserole.

In a saucepan, heat 2 tbs. of the butter over medium heat and sauté onions and bell pepper until softened. Stir in flour and sauté for 1 minute. Add milk and cheese, reduce heat to low and stir until cheese is melted and mixture is slightly thickened. Stir in salt and cayenne. Remove skillet from heat and pour cheese sauce over macaroni in casserole.

In a small nonstick skillet, heat remaining 1 tbs. butter over medium heat and sauté garlic with breadcrumbs for 2 minutes. Sprinkle breadcrumb mixture over macaroni and cheese sauce and sprinkle with Parmesan cheese. Bake uncovered for 20 minutes, or until hot and bubbly.

# SPINACH FETTUCCINE WITH ZUCCHINI AND GORGONZOLA

Servings: 5-6

*This lovely, rich entrée needs only a green salad and hot bread to round out the meal.*

10 oz. spinach fettuccine
2 tbs. canola oil
2 tbs. butter
4 cups diced zucchini or other summer
   squash

1½ cups sliced mushrooms
½ lb. Gorgonzola cheese, crumbled
1 cup half-and-half
red pepper flakes to taste
snipped fresh chives for garnish

In a large pot of boiling salted water, cook fettuccine according to package directions; drain and set aside. In a large skillet, heat oil and butter over medium heat and sauté zucchini and mushrooms just until crisp-tender. In a saucepan or in the top of a double boiler, melt cheese with half-and-half over low heat. Transfer cheese sauce to skillet with pasta and pepper flakes and toss well. Gently cook mixture until heated through. Transfer mixture to a warm serving platter or individual plates and garnish with snipped chives.

# SPINACH FETTUCCINE WITH YELLOW PEPPERS AND NUTS

*This makes a very pretty presentation accompanied by hot bread and a tomato salad. For company, you may wish to add a first-course soup.*

3 tbs. unsalted butter
2 tbs. olive oil
3 large cloves garlic, minced
3 large yellow bell peppers, seeded, ribs removed and cut into ¼-inch strips

12 oz. spinach fettuccine
1 cup freshly grated Parmesan cheese
½ cup pine nuts, toasted
½ cup walnut quarters, toasted

Bring a large pot of salted water to a boil. In a large skillet, heat butter and oil over medium heat and sauté garlic and bell peppers for 3 to 4 minutes, or until garlic is golden and peppers are crisp-tender; remove from heat.

Cook fettuccine in boiling water according to package directions; drain. Transfer fettuccine to skillet with pepper mixture and heat through, if necessary. Divide pasta mixture among 5 or 6 plates, sprinkling each portion with Parmesan cheese, pine nuts and walnuts. Serve immediately.

# FETTUCCINE WITH ZUCCHINI

*Fettuccine and zucchini always make a lovely combination. Accompany this with a fruit or green salad and whole grain bread.*

3 tbs. olive oil
1 medium onion, quartered and thinly sliced
1 tbs. minced garlic
2 cups sliced mushrooms
½ tsp. dried oregano leaves, crumbled
¼ tsp. fennel seeds
⅓ cup fresh flat-leaf parsley leaves
1 can (1 lb.) peeled plum tomatoes
¼ cup dry red wine
salt and freshly ground pepper to taste
1 lb. small zucchini, thinly sliced
10 oz. fettuccine
1 cup freshly grated Asiago cheese

Bring a large pot of salted water to a boil. In a large skillet, heat oil over medium heat and sauté onion for 3 minutes. Add garlic and sauté for 1 minute. Add mushrooms, oregano and fennel and sauté until mushrooms are softened and seasonings are fragrant. Stir in parsley, tomatoes and wine, breaking up mixture with a fork or your hand. Season lightly with salt and pepper. Cover skillet and simmer mixture over low heat for 20 minutes. Stir in zucchini and cook for 5 minutes.

Cook fettuccine in boiling water according to package directions; drain. Divide pasta among 6 warmed shallow bowls, top with sauce and sprinkle with cheese. Serve immediately.

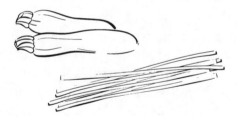

# VEGETABLE SPAGHETTI

*Serve this tasty pasta dish with a tomato soup or salad and freshly baked bread.*

3 tbs. olive oil
¼ cup minced garlic
1½ cups thin 2-inch-long zucchini strips
1 red bell pepper, seeded, ribs removed and
    cut into thin, 2-inch-long strips
¼ lb. mushrooms, sliced
8 oz. spaghetti
½ cup chopped fresh flat-leaf parsley leaves
1 cup grated Asiago cheese

Bring a large pot of salted water to a boil. In a 12-inch nonstick skillet, heat 2 tbs. of the oil over medium heat and sauté garlic for 1 minute. Add remaining 1 tbs. oil to skillet. Add zucchini, bell pepper and mushrooms and sauté for 4 to 5 minutes, or until vegetables are crisp-tender. Cover vegetables and keep warm.

Cook spaghetti in boiling water according to package directions; drain. Transfer cooked spaghetti and parsley to skillet with vegetables and toss well. Serve on plates and top with cheese.

# GARLICKY SPAGHETTI
# WITH PEPPER FLAKES

*Since this is a light dish, serve it with a filling, hot or cold soup and a hearty bread.*

8 oz. spaghetti
½ cup olive oil
3 tbs. minced garlic
½ tsp. red pepper flakes
salt to taste
freshly grated Parmesan cheese

In a large pot of boiling salted water, cook spaghetti according to package directions; drain.

While pasta is cooking, heat oil in a large skillet over medium heat and sauté garlic for 2 minutes. Stir in pepper flakes and remove from heat. Transfer drained cooked spaghetti to skillet, season lightly with salt and toss well. Pass Parmesan cheese at the table.

# FUSILLI WITH GREENS AND MUSHROOMS

*For the greens, choose collard greens or kale. Mustard greens can be used if they are young. This dish is well complemented by a tomato soup or salad and hot bread.*

1 lb. strong-flavored greens, well washed, tough stalks trimmed
12 oz. fusilli
1/3 cup olive oil
1 large onion, thinly sliced
1 tbs. minced garlic
1/2 lb. mushrooms, sliced
1/2 tsp. dried oregano leaves, crumbled
1/4 tsp. red pepper flakes
1 1/2 tbs. balsamic vinegar, or more to taste
salt to taste
freshly grated Parmesan cheese

Bring a large pot of salted water to a boil. Add greens to water and cook until tender, depending on the age and type of greens. With a slotted spoon, transfer greens to a colander. When slightly cool, chop greens coarsely. In same pot of boiling water, cook fusilli according to package directions; drain and set aside.

In a large skillet, heat oil over medium heat and sauté onion and garlic for 4 to 5 minutes. Add mushrooms, oregano and red pepper flakes and sauté until mushrooms are soft. Add chopped cooked greens, drained cooked fusilli, balsamic vinegar and salt and toss well. Pass Parmesan cheese at the table.

# FUSILLI WITH MARINATED TOMATOES

*A crowd-pleaser, this salad goes well with gazpacho or another chilled soup and whole grain rolls.*

12 oz. fusilli
1 jar (8 oz.) marinated sun-dried
   tomatoes packed in oil
½ cup white wine vinegar
¼ cup water
1 tbs. Worcestershire sauce
1 tsp. Dijon-style mustard
1 tbs. minced garlic

salt and freshly ground pepper to taste
1½ cups thinly sliced zucchini
1 small red onion, quartered and thinly
   sliced
½ cup fresh flat-leaf parsley leaves
2 cups tiny diced soft white cheese,
   such as teleme or fresh mozzarella

In a large pot of boiling salted water, cook fusilli according to package directions. Drain pasta, rinse with cool water and drain again; set aside. Drain oil from tomatoes into a large bowl. To bowl, add vinegar, water, Worcestershire, mustard and garlic. Whisk to mix well and season with salt and pepper. Chop sun-dried tomatoes into bite-sized pieces and add to bowl with fusilli, zucchini, onion, parsley and cheese; toss well.

# FRESH TOMATOES WITH OLIVES AND FUSILLI

*This is a lovely dish when tomatoes are ripe and basil is in season. Serve it preceded by a chilled soup and whole grain bread.*

¼ cup olive oil
2 tbs. minced garlic
1½ lb. fresh ripe tomatoes, cored,
   peeled, seeded and chopped
1½ cups halved kalamata olives

1 cup torn fresh basil leaves
salt and freshly ground pepper to taste
10 oz. fusilli
1½ cups crumbled feta cheese

In a small skillet, heat 2 tbs. of the oil over medium heat and sauté garlic until golden. Transfer garlic to a bowl with remaining 2 tbs. oil, tomatoes, olives and basil. Stir to mix well and let stand for at least 1 hour to blend flavors. Season lightly with salt and pepper.

At serving time, cook fusilli in a large pot of boiling salted water according to package directions; drain. In a nonstick skillet, cook tomato mixture until heated through. Transfer fusilli to skillet and toss well. Serve immediately topped with feta cheese.

# TOMATO AND ORZO SALAD

Servings: 5

*Tiny, teardrop-shaped orzo pasta works well in a lunch salad. In the summer, serve this dish for a light supper paired with soup and hot bread.*

10 oz. orzo
3 tbs. olive oil
3 medium-sized firm ripe tomatoes, cored, peeled, seeded and chopped
½ cup fresh flat-leaf parsley leaves
½ cup chopped kalamata olives
½ cup finely chopped sweet red onion
*Creamy Lemon Dressing*, page 53, to taste

In a large pot of boiling salted water, cook orzo according to package directions; do not overcook. Drain orzo, rinse with cool water and drain again. Transfer orzo to a bowl, fluff with a fork and toss with olive oil. To bowl, add tomatoes, parsley, olives and onion and toss well. Dress mixture lightly with *Creamy Lemon Dressing* and toss well. Cover salad and chill until almost ready to serve. Bring to room temperature before serving.

# INDEX

# Serve creative, easy, nutritious meals with nitty gritty® cookbooks

Wraps and Roll-Ups
Easy Vegetarian Cooking
Party Fare: Irresistible Nibbles for Every Occasion
Cappuccino/Espresso: The Book of Beverages
Fresh Vegetables
Cooking with Fresh Herbs
Cooking with Chile Peppers
The Dehydrator Cookbook
Recipes for the Pressure Cooker
Beer and Good Food
Unbeatable Chicken Recipes
Gourmet Gifts
From Freezer, 'Fridge and Pantry
Edible Pockets for Every Meal
Oven and Rotisserie Roasting
Risottos, Paellas and Other Rice Specialties
Muffins, Nut Breads and More
Healthy Snacks for Kids
100 Dynamite Desserts
Recipes for Yogurt Cheese
Sautés
Cooking in Porcelain

Casseroles
The Toaster Oven Cookbook
Skewer Cooking on the Grill
Creative Mexican Cooking
Marinades
No Salt, No Sugar, No Fat Cookbook
Quick and Easy Pasta Recipes
Cooking in Clay
Deep Fried Indulgences
The Garlic Cookbook
From Your Ice Cream Maker
The Best Pizza is Made at Home
The Best Bagels are Made at Home
Convection Oven Cookery
The Steamer Cookbook
The Pasta Machine Cookbook
The Versatile Rice Cooker
The Bread Machine Cookbook
The Bread Machine Cookbook II
The Bread Machine Cookbook III
The Bread Machine Cookbook IV: *Whole Grains & Natural Sugars*
The Bread Machine Cookbook V: *Favorite Recipes from 100 Kitchens*

The Bread Machine Cookbook VI: *Hand-Shaped Breads from the Dough Cycle*
Worldwide Sourdoughs from Your Bread Machine
Entrées from Your Bread Machine
The New Blender Book
The Sandwich Maker Cookbook
Waffles
The Coffee Book
The Juicer Book I and II
Bread Baking
The 9 x 13 Pan Cookbook
Recipes for the Loaf Pan
Low Fat American Favorites
Healthy Cooking on the Run
Favorite Seafood Recipes
New International Fondue Cookbook
Favorite Cookie Recipes
Cooking for 1 or 2
The Well Dressed Potato
Extra-Special Crockery Pot Recipes
Slow Cooking
The Wok

**For a free catalog, write or call: Bristol Publishing Enterprises, Inc.**
**P.O. Box 1737, San Leandro, CA 94577 (800) 346-4889**